Seville

Footprint

Andy Symington

Contents

Listings

About the author

Andy Symington is from Sydney, Australia. After studying some archaeology and psychology he became embroiled in the world of theatre administration and stage management. Moving into freelance journalism he lived in Edinburgh for two years selling whisky and wine and roaming the highlands before moving to northern Spain. Andy's first glimpse of the pointed hoods of Semana Santa was as a slightly unnerved six year old. Since that early memory he has returned many times to Seville over the years, has honed a healthy appetite for *manzanilla*, utterly failed to acquire the fundamentals of Andalucían horsemanship, and made valiant, but ultimately fruitless tilts at longstanding local tapas-eating records.

Travel is a passion and he has spent much time in South America and north Africa as well as Europe; he also enjoys prowling around his native land. He is author of Footprint Bilbao and Northern Spain and co-author of Footprint Spain.

Acknowledgements

Many thanks to tapas warrior Ben Hogan for whom one more *lomo* was never a bridge too far. Thanks also to Frank Swindells and Ruth Maldonado, fine after-dark guides to Sevilla, to Claire Boobbyer and the Footprint editorial team, to my parents and Riika Åkerlind for their support from down under, to David Jackson and Menchu Hevia, to the helpful staff of the Calle Arjona tourist office and especially to María, for whom every *caseta* had a welcome.

EL PACTO DE LA VICTORIA

Delving beyond the lovable icons; the flamenco, the oranges, the horse carriages, the haunting Semana Santa celebrations, you find – of course – a city. But what a city; a place where being seen is nothing unless you're seen to be having fun, where the musical traditions of gypsies cross dark eyes with the proud inheritances of Andalucían grandees, where people are united by tapas and divided by football and where the ghosts of Spain walk the streets, be they fictional, like Don Juan or Carmen or historical, like Cervantes or Columbus. A place described in the 16th century as having "the smell of a city and of something undefinable, of another greatness".

While the city's fortunes have waxed and waned, its allure has not; the census sheet bristles with travellers who came for a week and never left, while within Spain its name is spoken like a mantra, a word laden with sensuality and promise. Promise of the scent of desert peoples, of the scent of the Americas, of the scent of proud Castillian kings. Promise of the taste of fine food, of genuine welcome, vitality, and of inconclusive stories told over tapas and taximeters.

Set sail for the Spanish Main!

Unusually for an inland city, Seville was once the most important port in the world. It directed the whole of Spain's trade with its New World colonies and the merchants and Crown salivated over the arrival of the gold- and silver-laden treasure convoys fresh from its mines. The king's share was forged into coinage; the doubloons and pieces of eight that symbolized Spain's wealth and power, but in reality were quickly devoured by Genoese loan sharks or the pay packets of conscript soldiers fighting futile wars. The writing was on the wall and it all went wrong; the international hubbub faded as the country went bankrupt, the river silted up, the merchants disappeared and the plague culled the rest. But today, the bristling ramparts of the Torre del Oro still dare invaders to do their worst, while many of the streets of Triana, the one-time sailors' barrio, still bear the names of the brave mariners who set forth into the unknown. You can find spots where Columbus prayed before his voyages or the ill-fated Magellan set forth to put a girth on the world. The artistic and architectural legacies from these golden years are powerful and poignant reminders of limitless optimism brought about by what must have seemed a bottomless cup of bounty.

A Virgin's honour

In more religious cities, convents are places shrouded in mystery. Not so in Seville, where people drop in to them to buy nun-made pastries to have with their morning coffee. Although there's always plenty of pew room at the local church, religious institutions are still very much part of life in the city. Most marked is the extraordinary festival of Semana Santa. The Virgin figures in particular inspire deep adoration; people keep pictures of them in their wallets as they might of their partners and everyone has their favourite, whose perfection they will defend like their mothers' reputation. They'll often drop in to the chapel to check how she is and they'll chat about her qualities like they might a film star or a love interest. It's an affair that leaves the foreigner bemused and perhaps a little envious.

At a glance

The cathedral and around

The historic hub of Seville is dominated by two awesome symbols of power and wealth, the cathedral and Alcázar. Both hark back to the city's Moorish days; the one built over the old mosque, the other owing plenty to the architectural genius of *Al-Andalus*. Around is the bustle of horse carriages and the scent of orange blossom, while overlooking all is the Giralda, a sublime fantasy of brickwork that was once a minaret. More sober is the impartial Archive of the Indies, a Renaissance building that sits like a magistrate waiting to pass judgement on Spain's colonial history.

Barrio Santa Cruz

Much is made of Seville's Moorish and Jewish heritage, but finding it can be a frustrating business; an Arabic inscription here, the smell of blossom, the bustle of a market, the flash of dark eyes, but only ever glimpses. But it's still elusively alive among the narrow streets of this quarter. Push out into the lanes keeping your eyes open for interesting snippets. Once done, head over to the tapas area and do some exploration of a different kind. Under the orange trees of Calle Mateos Gago gazing at the Giralda while snacking on a spicy chickpea stew or a skewered lamb brochette, Moorish Spain may not seem so very far away. Banish the siren songs of history with a wedge of tortilla or pork *secreto* and a draught of *manzanilla* and you'll be back in Catholic Spain again.

South of the cathedral

The optimistic buildings erected for the 1929 Exhibition have been put to fine use; students bustle about between cafés and lectures and cityfolk stroll in the blessed shade of the Parque María Luisa, home to the improbably grand Plaza de España and two museums. The exhibition was a flop, as straitening financial circumstances kept tourists away, but it pushed Seville beyond the mental barriers of its old city walls and into the modern era. Among it all is the old tobacco factory, where Carmen once earned a crust.

El Arenal
Once the sandy, seedy, flood plain of the Guadalquivir, this area was built up around Seville's half-finished bullring. It's now one of the city's most interesting zones, liberally sprinkled with high-quality tapas bars. The riverside promenade with its terraces, palm trees, and swallows, makes a picturesque evening stroll as the sun sets over Triana and the Moorish Torre del Oro tower is evocatively lit.

Triana
The birthplace of flamenco in Seville, Triana's backstreet bars still have a lot to offer if you prowl around and keep your ears open. Once the home of transatlantic sailors, then gypsies, Triana is a little gentrified these days, but there's still a strong sense of community and a wealth of local characters. Home to most of Seville's chirpy *azulejo* tiles, this is the place to come to buy ceramics, or for a terraced dinner by the Guadalquivir. At night there's a lively bar and *discoteca* scene on the river, while the streets behind host Seville's most down-to-earth tapas scene.

Centro and San Vicente
A cluster of plazas and shopping streets fill the middle of Seville's old town. If you want to dress Sevillian, this is the place to come to kit yourself up with flamenca dress, shawl and comb or *traje de corto* horseman's wear – essential Feria fashion. If the wallet needs a break, calm down with a pastry in one of the city's iconic *pastelerías*, small Edens for the sweet of tooth. Tucked away in side streets are baroque churches, still in use by locals, who squeeze into the pews with their shopping bags on their way home. Follow them in and discover little-heralded masterpieces of painting and sculpture. For a bigger hit, head to quiet San Vicente and the Museo de Bellas Artes.

La Macarena

Seville's proud anarchist traditions are still alive in this large barrio, still hemmed in by a long and impressive stretch of the Muslim city walls. If lively, friendly local bars are your preferred night-time destination, you'll want to give the Alameda de Hércules plenty of attention, while by day you'll be drawn by the lively Thursday and Sunday morning markets and the quiet lanes brimming with Gothic-Mudéjar convents and churches. Pride of place goes to the city's most famous resident; visit her in her own modern basilica where the beautiful Virgen de la Macarena weeps jewelled tears for the death of her Son.

Isla de la Cartuja

This river island was completely redeveloped as the site of the 1992 World Expo. Now home to a good theme park, a couple of museums and a handful of university faculties, it's got a slightly sad air of dereliction as many of the innovative buildings that once hosted 15 million visitors decay through disuse, but it is undeniably interesting for its architecture and also for its monastery where Columbus once prayed. Sensitive to trends, it made itself useful as a ceramics factory when monks went out of fashion and daringly re-emerged as a good modern art gallery after its role as the Royal Pavilion in the Exposition.

New Town Boulevards

Although you'll spend most of your time in the old town, much of Seville actually lives out in the new suburbs, partitioned by long, elegant avenues. Home to Seville's football clubs, who regularly bury the hatchet right where it's going to hurt most, it's also a good zone for *discotecas* and bars. It's a well-planned modern urban space, with some sound modern buildings, such as the Santa Justa train station, and relaxing public spaces like the Jardines de la Buhaira.

Trip planner

When to go to Seville depends partly on how much money you want to spend. Heading over for Easter's Semana Santa or the April Feria is an excellent experience but you'll pay nearly double for accommodation, more for drinks and food, and you'll find few bars serving tapas (at least in Semana Santa). Visiting in other parts of spring or in autumn is a good bet as the weather will still be hot, but not overpowering, as it is in July and August, when most Sevillians get out of town themselves and things are eerily quiet. Winter's not a bad time to visit either; prices are down, and temperatures comfortable, but you'll miss the terraces and outdoor socializing that are an essential part of Seville life. But it's a magical city at any time of the year and even the heat can be endured with well-timed siestas, cheap taxi rides, visits to air-conditioned museums or a sly sherry on a shady terrace.

24 hours

With only a day, you should confine yourself to the Alcázar and cathedral (or the Museo de Bellas Artes), both of which take a fair portion of time to appreciate. Have a wander around Barrio Santa Cruz too and find somewhere to have lunch before hitting El Arenal for some great tapas in the evening. See some flamenco, either at a *tablao* or one of the bars that puts it on regularly; if you fancy kicking on, cross over to Triana, or for a more alternative scene, head for the Alameda de Hércules. Don't kill yourself sightseeing though; eating and drinking in Seville is perhaps its supreme charm.

A long weekend

With more time at your disposal, make sure you give the Alcázar, cathedral, and Museo de Bellas Artes all the time that they need. The Hospital de Caridad can be seen in a relatively quick visit, and the Casa de Pilatos is an excellent example of a Renaissance palace. Definitely fit in an afternoon in the Parque María Luisa and its

★ **Ten of the best**

Best

1   Real Alcázar A superb fusion of architectural styles, this elegant palace is still home to visiting royalty and not to be missed. Take a book or a picnic and while away a few hours in its superb gardens, p38.

2   La Catedral A Gothic magnificence whose chapels secrete hundreds of artistic masterpieces. The lofty Giralda tower is sublime, especially at night, p33.

3   Ayuntamiento Only open a couple of times a week, it's worth going in to see the superb stone-carved rooms, all the better for still being in daily use, p79.

4   Hospital de la Caridad If you're opening a hospital and want the chapel decorated, it helps if you're good friends with two of the city's finest ever painters, p60.

5   The excellent, facing, museums of **Archaeology** and **Popular Customs**, perfectly set in the shade of Parque María Luisa, p55.

6   El Faro de Triana Superb location, river views, incredibly cheap and generous tapas bar. See if you can cross the bridge without popping in, p137.

7   Museo de Bellas Artes For a century, Seville produced some of the finest of European art. And a lot of it's here, p75.

8   Staying up all night on Maundy Thursday to watch the finest of the city's **Semana Santa processions**, then a hot chocolate and pastry before crawling off to bed, p170.

9   Dancing *sevillanas* in a caseta at **Feria** after watching Seville parading in their horse carriages and having knocked back a few *manzanillas*, p66.

10   Trying to squeeze in a *montadito de pringá* after a lengthy **tapas crawl** through Barrio Santa Cruz, El Arenal, or Triana.

museums and make sure you also stroll through Triana, perhaps dining in a waterside restaurant such as *La Primera del Puente* (see p136). If the *Ayuntamiento* is open, fit that in as well; you won't regret it. Spend an hour one evening on a riverboat cruise as you'll see parts of the city that you may not have had time to get to otherwise. Whatever your schedule, make sure you pace the streets of Barrio Santa Cruz and El Arenal at least once.

With four days, you may want to plan a day trip to Córdoba and its fabulous Mezquita or Jerez and its sherry bodegas. The Roman ruins at Itálica can comfortably be visited in half a day as can the pretty town of Carmona.

A week

If you're a lover of art, you'll want to spend plenty of time in the cathedral and Museo de Bellas Artes, as well the Hospital de Caridad and also spend some time hunting down paintings in some of Seville's lesser-known churches such as Santa María La Blanca or La Magdalena. You should spend plenty of strolling hours exploring the barrios of Triana and La Macarena and their churches, and you should be able to name at least half a dozen good bars in all the major tapas zones by the end of your stay. Make sure you plan in a visit to the *Ayuntamiento* and catch a bullfight or a football game if you fancy it. See both museums in the Parque de María Luisa and spend some time trying to track down some elusive, authentic flamenco as well as visiting a more established venue. You'll be able to visit both Córdoba and Jerez or perhaps one of the lesser-known gems such as Ecija with its baroque belltowers. If you're not there during Semana Santa, try and see some of the sculptures in their home churches to get an idea of what it's all about; El Cachorro, La Esperanza de Triana, La Macarena, and Jesús del Gran Poder are recommended. And make sure you spend at least an hour a day doing nothing while sipping a *café con hielo* (coffee poured over ice) on a terrace somewhere. If you haven't idled in the heat, you can't claim to know Seville.

Contemporary Seville

It's the 21st century, the EU is expanding and the capital of one of the union's largest administrative regions has plenty on its plate. While the old centre continues to delight and astonish visitors and the locals keep the good-time flags flying in the bars and cafés, the government has social and economic problems that it will have to tackle without being cut as much Euro-slack as before. For Seville, as for other Spanish cities, the post-Franco honeymoon is over.

While some semi-autonomous communities have unquestionably thrived since their creation, it was always going to be a bumpy ride for Andalucía. With massive unemployment (unfairly perceived by the rest of Spain as an unwillingness to work in the summer heat, although a wander around Seville's cafés certainly can give that impression) and a lack of a modern commercial or industrial infrastructure, plenty of Seville has been doing it tough for years, although it's not immediately visible to the visitor. This is exacerbated by a skewed distribution of wealth that has been in place since the *Reconquista*. While many *sevillanos* have bullfight season tickets and a horse and carriage for Feria in the garage, there's a worrying number of homeless people, substantial desperate immigration into a city poorly equipped to cope with it and seedy suburbs where heroin enlivens life on the Spanish fringes.

Some of these problems have existed for centuries; flamenco, the music of the gypsies with its dark tragic themes, is a reflection of this, as are the city's Virgins of the traditionally working-class barrios of La Macarena and Triana, literally symbols of hope in more troubled times, and still adored fervently now.

Seville's saviour has been tourism. While the 1992 World Expo incurred massive debts, corruption was rife and the site now stands in semi-dereliction, it did help place Seville even more firmly on the map as a destination and major infrastructural improvements were implemented. Modern architecture received a much-needed boost and the city was graced with many new buildings, from the emblematic Calatrava bridges, the Andalucían Junta and the Teatro de la Maestranza to more humble libraries, office blocks, and apartments which, while they may lack the panache of a Guggenheim, are to be particularly admired for the way they have slotted into the historic cityscape.

While Expo undoubtedly boosted tourism, it wasn't a marketing gimmick. Visitors have been coming since the early 19th century, unable to keep the smiles off their faces confronted with the leisurely life, the superb tapas and stunning ensembles of painting, sculpture and architecture.

The people of Seville are another attraction. Their beauty is a fact that has been endlessly commented and quoted on and their openness and amiability, legendary. It is inaccurate, however, to categorize them so easily. Architecturally, the Seville house has traditionally been an inverted structure built around a central patio; a half-open door offering a glimpse of what lies within. Something of the same desire for privacy is in the personalities of Sevillians too. While a stranger in the bar will happily chat about politics or football, they won't volunteer information about themselves and you can feel very honoured indeed if you are invited to their house. It's perhaps best summed up by a quote from a *sevillana* dancer. "We love it when people from outside Seville come here and dance, and we'll happily dance with them. They'll enjoy it, they'll feel excitement and exhilaration, but they won't understand it. Not even if they're from Cádiz or Córdoba. You have to grow up with it to understand". A reflection on a culture far deeper than first-time observation might reveal.

When people from English-speaking backgrounds talk of "the finer things in life" they generally mean those things that give them pleasure. A *sevillano* would say it the other way around; a night spent in the company of friends, a good meal, a leisurely coffee on a sunny *terraza*, a puff on a good cigar, a night of dancing until you've no energy left; these are not the finer things, these are the basics, and the rest of life must be planned so that they remain so. This is

Stacked up
Torero and bull compete on the postcard
stand as they do in La Maestranza
on fight days.

the attitude that attracted 19th-century visitors; Merimée, who penned Carmen for example and is an essential part of Seville's charm. The homogenization of modern European life and dumbed-down media culture has affected this, but far from fatally; it's still a blessed relief to get off a plane from London or Frankfurt and notice that everyone walks at half the pace and still gets everything done. The tapas culture is a good example of this. For visitors, what impresses is the quality of the food and the sheer "civilizedness" of it; for Sevillians it's a logical and enjoyable way to spend time with friends, chat to barkeepers, and have a meal and a few drinks at the same time.

Politically, Seville has always been a polarized place. The birth-place of the CNT anarchists, it was also fertile recruiting ground for the Falange in the 30s. Culturally, it's strongly conservative, which is a double-edged sword. While the horse carriages, fans, castanets and *nazarenos* have become Spanish icons, the city isn't one you'd back to produce the next revolution in popular culture. The fact that the best known song to come out of the city is *Macarena*, a clichéd tune produced by an ancient pair of musical has-beens, tells a story (as does its worldwide popularity, mind you). There's little variation in the contemporary music scene and almost no live bands. In some ways, flamenco takes a lot of the talent and energy that would otherwise be diverted elsewhere. Other art forms struggle a little; not much money is channelled into them and the theatre-going scene remains reactionary.

Social and cultural problems aside though, what is most attractive about Seville is the general air of contentment. *Sevillanos* are always at pains to convince visitors what a pleasant place it is; completely unnecessarily, as most people have already formed that impression after a couple of hours. It's a happy place and people enjoy living in it, actually something that can be said about precious few European cities. The Metro is currently under construction in the city and it will be like no other in the world. In Seville people are going to talk on the underground.

By far the best way of getting to Seville is by air; fares are usually reasonable from the rest of Europe, and you can always bag a cheap charter to Málaga, which is not too far away on the bus. If you're just visiting Seville, don't take the motor; it's not a car-friendly city.

The city is very easy to get around; most sights of interest are encompassed within the area once enclosed by some of the most formidable walls in Europe. It's just about all walkable, although resorting to buses and taxis is sometimes a godsend in the baking sun.

High season in Seville terms is March to May; this period encompasses the most pleasant weather and the two major festivals, Semana Santa and Feria de Abril. Prices are notably higher during this time. Summer is a quiet time as temperatures rise to almost unbearable levels (52°C in 2003); autumn is a good time to visit, and winter is much milder here than in other parts of Europe.

Getting there

Air

From the UK and Ireland There are daily direct flights to Seville with Iberia and British Airways from London Heathrow and Gatwick, as well as numerous opportunities for connections via Madrid and Barcelona. The cost of a return trip is about £150-230 depending on season and prebooking. Flight time is around 2 hours 40 minutes non-stop from London. **Easy Value** is a good internet flight comparison service, while **Opodo** is an efficient engine for searching Europe's major airlines. A reasonable cheap option is the **Ryanair** flight from London Stansted to Jerez, which operates only on Saturdays and Sundays. Fares can fall as low as £50 return, but are usually £130 or more. Jerez is regularly linked by train and bus to Seville (1 hour). Málaga is one of the easiest airports in Spain to get to cheaply from the UK, and the city is 2½ hours from Seville by bus (hourly). As well as **Easyjet**, **Virgin Express**, and **BMI**, there are numerous charter flights from many British and Irish airports. These flights can fall as low as £80 return out of season, but are normally £120-150 in spring and summer. **Avro** is one of the best charter flight companies, but be sure to check the travel pages of newspapers for cheap deals. If you can pick up a cheap flight to Madrid (such as on Easyjet), you can get to Seville and back on the bus (€15 each way, 6 hours), but getting the fast train will wipe out any saving.

From Europe There are daily non-stop flights to Seville from Paris Orly (3 a day, operated by **Air France/Iberia**) and from Brussels (**SN Brussels Airlines**). These fares tend to hover around €250-300 but can be substantially lower with offers or out of season. Flying from these or other western European cities via Madrid or Barcelona is usually about the same. Cheaper flights can be got to such places as Málaga (many charter companies; 2½ hours from Seville by bus), Jerez (**Ryanair** via London, see above),

→ Airlines and travel agents

Air Europa, www.air-europa.com
Airfare.com, www.airfare.com
Air France, www.airfrance.com
American Airlines, www.aa.com
Avro, www.avro.com
BMI, www.flybmi.com
British Airways, www.britishairways.com
Delta, www.delta.com
Dial a Flight, www.dialaflight.com
Easyjet, www.easyjet.com
Easy Value, www.easyvalue.com
ebookers, www.ebookers.com
Expedia, www.expedia.co.uk; www.expedia.com
Iberia, www.iberia.es
Lastminute.com, www.lastminute.com
Opodo, www.opodo.com
Ryanair, www.ryanair.com
SN Brussels Airlines, www.flysn.com
Spanair, www.spanair.com
Virgin Express, www.virginexpress.com

or Madrid (**Easyjet** via London, or **Virgin Express** via Brussels).
For internal Spanish flights, check the **Iberia** website for
last-minute specials or local travel agents – special offers can bring
a Barcelona-Seville flight down to about € 80 return if you're
lucky, but expect to pay double that. There are six daily flights from
both Barcelona and Madrid.

From North America There are no direct flights from North America to Seville, so you will have to connect via Madrid, Barcelona, London, or another European city. From the east coast, flights can rise to more than US$1000 in summer, but in winter, or with advance purchase, you can get away with as little as US$500. Prices from the west coast are usually only US$100 or so more. **Iberia** flies direct to Madrid from many east coast cities, and **British Airways** often offers reasonable add-on fares via London. You can save considerably by flying to Madrid and getting the bus to Seville (€15 each way, 6 hours).

Airport Information Seville's airport (SVQ) is located 10 kilometres northeast of the centre. Modernized by the successful Navarran architect Rafael Moneo, the interior welcomes visitors with orange trees. There are the usual facilities, including a tourist information kiosk (except left luggage; this can be done at the train station or either bus station) and several car hire companies. A bus runs to and from the airport to central Seville (Puerta de Jerez) via the train and bus stations. It goes roughly every 30 minutes weekdays and is designed to coincide with international flights. It takes 30 minutes to Puerta de Jerez. There are fewer at weekends; a one-way fare is €2.10. The last bus leaves the airport at 2330, well after the last flight has got in. There are plenty of taxis; a fare to the city is currently € 21 during the day, slightly more at night or on public holidays.

Car

Seville is more than 2000 kilometres from London by road; a dedicated drive will get you there in 20-24 driving hours. By far the fastest route is to head down the west coast of France to Madrid via Bilbao then south via Córdoba. Cars must be insured for third party and practically any driving licence is acceptable (but if you're from a place that a Guardia Civil would struggle to locate on a map, take an International Driving Licence). Tolls on motorways in France and Northern Spain will add significantly to your costs; petrol costs €0.80-0.90 per litre in Spain. Driving conditions in Spain are very good, but negotiating Seville itself by car isn't pretty and foreign plates are a magnet to thieves.

Coach

The quickest way to get to Seville from Britain by bus is with **Eurolines** (www.eurolines.co.uk) to Madrid, then an interurban bus to Seville (15 each way, 6 hours). The London-Madrid sector takes 26-28 hours and costs around £120 return, although this can fall to £72 if booked a month in advance out of season. Eurolines also run a Paris-Seville service, while **Anibal** runs a Lisbon-Seville service that takes 6½ hours, €28. Seville is very well connected by interurban buses within Spain.

Train

Unless you've got a railpass or you are not too keen on planes, forget about getting to Seville by train from anywhere further than France; you'll save no money over the plane fare and use up days of time better spent in tapas bars. You will have to connect via either Barcelona (3 trains daily, 10-12 hours, €48.50-66.50) or Madrid (10-21 **AVE** fast trains daily, 2 hours 25 minutes, €64). Getting to Madrid/Barcelona from London takes about a day using **Eurostar** (www.eurostar.com, **T** 0870 160 6600); if you can't score a special offer count on £100-200 return to Paris, and another €130 or more return to reach Madrid/Barcelona from there. Using the ferry across the channel adds eight or more hours and saves up to £100.

Getting around

Bus

Seville's fleet of orange **TUSSAM** local buses runs a good service around the city. A single fare is €0.90 (drivers will give change up to a point), but you can buy a *bonobus* from many newspaper kiosks; this costs €4.50 and is valid for 10 journeys. TUSSAM's official kiosks are in Plaza Nueva; from here you can buy *tarjetas turísticas* that give you up to five journeys a day for a three or seven day period. The kiosks are open Monday-Friday 0900-1345, 1700-1900. Plaza Nueva is a hub for buses going to the south of the city, while Plaza Encarnación is the main one for buses going north and east. In practice, you're unlikely to use buses all that much, as the centre is pretty walkable. The most useful ones are the circular routes; buses C1 and C2 run a large circle via the train station and Expo site (C1 goes clockwise, C2 anticlockwise), while C3 (clockwise) and C4 (anticlockwise) follow the perimeter of the old walls, except for C3's brief detour into Triana. Other useful buses include the 13 running from Plaza del Duque to the Puerta de la Macarena via the Alameda de Hércules, the 40 running from Plaza Nueva into and around Triana, and the 32 from Plaza de la Encarnación to the train station. Buses for destinations outside Seville leave from one of two bus stations, the Prado de San Sebastián (for south and east), and Plaza de Armas (for west and north).

Car

Seville is not a great place to have a car. The narrow one-way streets of the old town, the impossibility of parking on the street, and the confusing layout don't make for a great experience. Car crime is low-key but significant, so you are taking a fair risk by parking your car above ground during your stay; leave nothing of value in the vehicle and open the glovebox. There are plenty of underground car parks that cost about €1 per hour/€15 per day and most hotels have a car park or an arrangement with a local one. There is a riverside car park by the Torre del Oro and plenty of parking among the buildings around the back of the old tobacco factory, but it's far from secure. If you are parking on the street, blue lines indicate pay-and-display zones (operational 0900-1400, 1600-2000; you can feed the meter for up to 2 hours); check signs

Travel extras

Safety On a western-European scale, Seville is a very safe place. Muggings are rare but not unheard of, as are alcohol-fuelled incidents at weekends, where young locals may try and mark their turf at the expense of (mostly) groups of foreign males. It's extremely unlikely, but keep your wits about you, especially around *discotecas*.

Tipping Locals generally leave nothing or small change in cafés and bars and waiters don't expect a tip. If the service is good in restaurants, 5% is customary and 10% is generous. Taxi drivers don't expect tips but it's common to round off the fare.

for other restrictions. Car hire isn't cheap; expect to pay €40 plus per day (less for a week). The process is fairly painless; you'll need a credit card, home driving licence, and be over 21 (25 for some companies). All the multinationals are present, as well as several local companies. See Car hire, Directory, for a list.

Cycling

Seville is not an especially cycle-friendly city; drivers have little respect for their two-wheeled brethren, and, apart from in the newer suburbs, there are few cycle lanes. That said, there are several areas that are good territory to explore by bike: the Parque María Luisa, the Isla de la Cartuja, and the Parque del Alamillo. Locals use scooters extensively, a practical option given the traffic jams and narrow streets of the old town. Theft of both these and bicycles is significant. There are several places to hire bikes, scooters and motorbikes. See Cycle hire, Directory, for details.

Taxi

Taxis are a good way to get around Seville, particularly with heavy bags in the summer heat. A green light is lit on top if they are available, and flagfall is a very reasonable €2. A ride right across town, for example from the cathedral to the Puerta de Macarena, or Triana to the train station, will cost €5-6. Prices rise slightly after 2200 and during fiestas such as Semana Santa or Feria.

Train

Seville has two short-distance Cercanía train lines (the one to Isla Cartuja is currently closed). These are of little use to the traveller unless you are visiting some of the towns around Seville such as Cazalla or Utrera. Their hub is the Santa Justa train station, which is the point of departure for all trains including those to Córdoba and Jerez. Seville's trams disappeared in 1960, but a gleaming new form of transport is currently being created; the eagerly awaited Metro. There's already a dummy station to allow Sevillians to get used to the ticket machines and underground feeling, but the first of the three lines won't open until 2005.

Walking

Most of Seville's sights of interest are in the old town. As it was once one of the biggest cities in Europe however, this is a fairly large area. Notwithstanding, walking is by far the best way to get around this area, large sections of which are pedestrianized. In the fierce spring and summer heat, or if you're trying to squeeze a lot of sightseeing in, making use of the circular bus routes and/ or taxis will save exhaustion. If you've got more time, do it on foot; it's a fascinating city to walk around. Don't bank on your laser-sharp sense of direction, however; not even most locals know the shortest route between two given points with any confidence. A stroll from the cathedral to the Museo de Bellas Artes will take 15-20 minutes, from the Plaza de España to the Alameda de Hércules about 30 minutes.

Tours

Boat tours

Cruceros Turisticos Torre del Oro, Muelle Torre del Oro s/n, **T** 954 561 692. A good cruise on the Guadalquivir, departing every 30 minutes from 1100 to dusk (except 1130) from the quay by the Torre del Oro. The boat travels both ways along the river and points out sights of interest; including the old quays where Ferdinand Magellan and others once set sail. Bar on board. €12, cruise lasts for an hour. The same company also runs summer cruises to the mouth of the river at Sanlúcar de Barrameda. Leaving at 0830 and returning at 2200, the trip costs €23 (kids up to 14 are €11). There are good birdwatching opportunities as the boat tracks past the edge of the Coto Doñaña wetlands, and you have four hours in Sanlúcar to have lunch and visit a manzanilla *bodega*. Tours begin in mid May at weekends only and increase in frequency through summer.

Bus tours

Sevilla Tour & Tour por Sevilla, **T** 902 101 081, **T** 954 560 693. Two almost identical double-decker bus tours of the city run by different Europe-wide companies. Both leave from the Torre del Oro every 30 minutes or so from 1000 and have the same four stops and hop-on, hop-off system, free walking tour, and tour of the 1929 expo site. They cost €12, but it's worth bargaining and checking for special promotions. Commentary is available in multiple languages.

Taxi tours

T 629 540 592, **T** 620 173 420. These run for 75 minutes in a Seville cab with comments on CD in English and Spanish. You can do them any time between 0900-2100 and (depending on the meter) cost about €20; they take up to four people.

Walking tours

Carmen Tour. A very good walking tour run by a Belgian Carmen lookalike who takes you through the sites relevant to the operatic heroine's story, throwing in a wealth of information on Seville on the way, accompanied by her own songs. It leaves from the Plaza del Triunfo at 1800 daily except Tuesday and Thursday. It lasts 90 minutes and payment is by donation; €5-10 seems fair.

Walking Tours of Sevilla, T 954 500 105, T 670 625 353. A two-hour walking tour of the city is €10 and leaves Monday-Saturday at 0930 (English) and 1130 (Spanish); the same company also runs tours of the Alcázar and cathedral (both €6 plus entry).

The Way of the Kings and **The Old Jewish Quarter**, T 680 436 629, are two good guided walks, the former starting daily at the Puerta de la Macarena at 1100, the latter in the Patio de Banderas at 1230. Phoning in advance essential.

Leyendas Sevillanas, T 678 570 188, www.leyendassevillanas.com, is an enjoyable 90-minute trip that combines a guided walk with interactive theatre enacting legends of the city's past. Check the webpage for upcoming performances; most are in Spanish, but there are some in English, and they can be arranged for groups. €10 per person.

Other tours

Horse Carriages. These can be found everywhere, particularly near the cathedral. Seating up to five, they'll take you on a pleasant trot around the city; you can specify which things you particularly want to see. Rates vary in season, and bargaining is useful; maximum tariffs currently stand at €36 per hour, rising to €72 in Feria; they're posted at the rank in the Plaza Virgen de los Reyes. Drivers provide a commentary of dubious accuracy.

Taberna de Alabardero, T 954 293 081, www.esh.es, is one of Seville's best restaurants and a famous hospitality school. It runs regular themed cooking weekends, usually running for 3 consecutive evenings. They cost €120-140.

Toros Tours, **T** 955 664 261, www.torostours.com Offers tours from Seville to ranches where fighting bulls are bred and to stud farms where the famous Andalucían horses are trained.

Tourist Information

The **Junta de Andalucía** runs the handiest tourist office, just near the cathedral on Av de la Constitución, **T** 954 221 404. Cursory rather than courtesy is the word that springs to mind, but to be fair, they are usually pretty busy. Open Monday-Friday 0900-1900, Saturday 1000-1400, 1500-1900, Sunday 1000-1400.

City tourist offices with better opening hours can be found by the Puente de Triana at C Arjona 28, **T** 902 194 897, Monday-Friday 0800-2045, Saturday-Sunday 0900-1400; and Paseo de las Delicias 9 (in a former gatehouse known as the "queen's sewing room"), **T** 954 234 465, Monday-Sunday 0800-1800. Both are friendly and the former is exceptionally well-informed.

There are also information booths at the airport and Santa Justa train station. Monday-Friday 0900-2000, Saturday-Sunday 1000-1400; the latter gives good information on other Andalucían destinations.

Useful maps

The free map given out by tourist offices isn't bad, but the Corte Inglés one that you find in hotel lobbies is a little better. It is worth picking up one with a street index, however; one of the best is the Castillejo edition available in most bookshops.

The cathedral and around 33

Muslim and Christian architecture dazzlingly combine.

Barrio Santa Cruz 43

Winding streets of the one-time Jewish quarter.

South of the cathedral 50

Pavilions of the 1929 Exhibition and tobacco factory.

El Arenal 56

Riverside area now home to bullfighting, theatre, tapas and the fine art of the Hospital de la Caridad.

Triana 63

Its trendified riverbank is a mass of bars and restaurants; its backstreets are full of beautiful tiles.

Centro and San Vicente 70

The centre is a busy mix of people. There are several excellent churches as well as a superb art gallery.

La Macarena 80

Working-class district full of interesting churches and chapels as well as most of the alternative scene.

Isla de la Cartuja 86

This river island was the site of World Expo 1992.

New Town Boulevards 89

Site for much of the commercial and residential life.

The cathedral and around

The vast Gothic cathedral and the sumptuous Mudéjar Alcázar,
Seville's bases of ecclesiastical and royal power, face each other
across the sunbeaten Plaza del Triunfo, once just inside the city's
*major gateway. The **cathedral** has more artistic masterpieces than*
*many major galleries as well as the emblematic **Giralda tower**, a*
*fantasy in ornate brickwork, while the **Alcázar**, the seat of generations*
of Moorish and Castillian kings, has breathtakingly beautiful patios,
portals and inlaid ceilings to rival Granada's Alhambra, as well as
acres of lush gardens. Between the two buildings is the comparatively
*understated **Archivo de las Indias**, currently closed but repository of*
tens of millions of pages of documents relating to Spain's imperial past.
In the squares, pretty horse carriages sit under the orange trees ready to
trot visitors around the sights of the town.

▸▸ *See Sleeping p127, Eating and drinking p127, Bars and clubs p149*

◉ Sights

★ La Catedral

Plaza del Triunfo s/n, **T** 954 214 971. *Mon-Sat 1100-1800 (last entry*
at 1700); Sun 1430-1900 (last entry at 1800). €6/1.50 students/free
Sun. The audio guide at €3 isn't particularly informative; you're better
off sticking to the display panels or buying a cathedral guide at the
shop here. Bus 40. Map 2, E3, p250

The fall of Seville to the Christians in 1248 was an event of massive
resonance. While Granada's capitulation in 1492 marked the final
victory, it was something of a foregone conclusion – the fall of
Seville really represented the breaking of the backbone of Muslim
Spain. After a while, at the beginning of the 15th century, the
Castillians decided to hammer home the point and erect a
cathedral over the mosque (which they had been using as a

church, on a scale that would leave no doubts that future generations would "think the architects mad". Santa María de la Sede is the result: a Gothic edifice of staggering proportions and crammed so full of artistic treasures that most of its chapels and altars could have been tourist attractions in their own right; there are nearly fifty of them.

Several Moorish elements were happily left standing; the city's symbol, the superb Giralda tower, is the most obvious of these. Originally the minaret of the mosque, it was built by the Almohads in the late-12th century and was one of the tallest buildings in the world in its day. Although rebuilt by the Christians after its destruction in an earthquake in 1356, its superb exterior brick decoration is true to the original, although the weathervane atop the structure (El Giraldillo) is not.

Approaching the cathedral for the first time, try and start from Plaza de San Francisco. Taking Calle Hernando Colón, another Moorish feature will soon become apparent – the Puerta de Perdón gateway with fine stucco decoration and a dogtoothed horseshoe arch. Turning left and walking around the whole structure will let you appreciate the Giralda and the many fine 15th-century Gothic doorways. You enter via the Puerta San Cristobal, next to the Archivo de las Indias. The first chamber is a small museum with several excellent pieces: a San Fernando by Bartolomé Esteban Murillo, and a Francisco Zurbarán depicting the Baptist in the desert; among others.

Around the chapels Once into the cathedral proper, after catching your breath at the dimensions and the pillars like trunks of an ancient stone forest, turn hard left and do a circuit of the chapels. Don't forget to look up once in a while to appreciate the lofty Gothic grandeur and the excellent stained glass, much of it by Heinrich of Germany (15th century) and Arnao of Flanders (16th century). At the western end of the church, Murillo's Guardian Angel stands to the left of the middle door, leading the Christ child by the hand. In the corner stands the much-darned 13th-century standard of Fernando III, which he flew from the Giralda when he conquered the city. Turning onto the north side, see if you can barge through the tour groups into the chapel of San Antonio, with a huge and much-admired Murillo of that saint's vision of a cloud of cherubs and angels. Above it is a smaller Baptism by the same artist. A Renaissance baptismal font here is still in use, while a 15th-century frieze of saints adorns the *reja* (screen). These *rejas* are works of art in their own right – some of them take wrought iron to extraordinary delicacy.

Arriving in the northeast corner, climb the Giralda. You reach the top via 35 ramps. These were designed to allow a horse to make it up. The tower is 94 m high and the view from the top is excellent. There's a host of bells up here; the oldest date from the 14th century. Coming down, the next chapel is that of St Peter and contains a *retablo* (altarpiece) with nine good Zurbaráns devoted to the life of the first pope, depicted here with a salt 'n' pepper beard. The superb Royal Chapel is often curtained off for services. The cuissons of its domed ceiling contain busts of kings and queens of Castilla. In a funerary urn are the remains of the beatified conqueror-king Fernando III, while his wife Beatrice of Swabia (the inspiration behind the Burgos cathedral) and their son Alfonso X (the Wise) are also buried here.

In the southeast corner, the treasury is entered through the Mariscal Chapel which has a stunning altarpiece centred on the Purification of Mary and painted by Pedro de Campaña, a Flemish artist of exalted talent. The treasury contains a display of monstrances (one of which holds a spine from the Crown of Thorns), salvers and processional crowns. A fine antechamber and courtyard adjoin the Chapterhouse with vault paintings by Murillo. The massive vestry is almost a church in its own right with an

! Guinness ranks Seville's cathedral the biggest in the world
• by volume, but then St Peter's in Rome and Notre Dame de
la Paix in the Côte d'Ivoire are basilicas, not cathedrals.

The potter saints

It is appropriate that Seville's two patron saints should have been involved in ceramics production. Justa and Rufina, two potters, were on their way home from market in the early days of Christianity in Seville in the late-3rd century AD. They were stopped by a pagan procession and the men carrying the idol demanded a donation from the two young women. They refused, saying they were Christians, whereupon the pagans smashed all their pots. In retaliation, they toppled the idol, shattering it on the ground. The girls were put to death for sacrilege; Rufina was burned alive, while Justa, who had died in prison, was stuffed down a well. The bishop retrieved her body and buried it with ceremony in a cemetery where the railway station named after her now stands. The two martyrs were named patrons of the city and quickly canonized.

ornate Plateresque entrance and three altars featuring fine paintings; a superb Descent from the Cross by Pedro de Campaña, a Santa Teresa by Zurbarán and a San Laurencio by Jordán. Two Murillos face each other across the room, they depict two of the city's earliest archbishops from the Visigothic period, San Isidoro and San Leandro. A huge silver monstrance is also present here, as are a number of treasures, including two fragments of the True Cross embedded in golden crucifixes, and the keys of the city said to have been handed over to the conquering Fernando; they are intricately engraved with Arabic and Hebrew lettering. After the chapel of St Andrew, the Chapel of Sorrows leads to the chalice vestry with its Goya painting of the city's patron saints Justa and Rufina flanking the Giralda. Christopher Columbus' tomb stands proud in the centre of the southern central doorway, borne aloft by four figures representing the kingdoms of Castilla, León, Aragón and Navarra. It's in late-19th century Romantic style and some remains were deposited there in 1902, but nobody knows for sure whose they are – Seville is one of four cities that claims to have the explorer's tomb. Columbus spent time praying in the next chapel which features an excellent 14th-century fresco of the Virgin, in the place where the mosque's mihrab once stood. The later retablo was built around the painting.

The Centre The cathedral's principal devotional spaces are in the centre of the massive five-naved structure – the choir and the chancel. The choir itself is closed off by a superb gilt Plateresque *reja* depicting the Tree of Jesse, while the ornate stalls feature misericords with charismatic depictions of demons and the vices. The main *retablo* is a marvel of Christian art and has been the subject of several books in its own right. Measuring a gigantic 18 m by 28 m, it was masterminded by the Flemish artist Pieter Dancart, who began it in 1481 and several other notable painters and sculptors worked on it until its completion in 1526. It is surmounted by a gilt canopy, atop which is a Calvary scene and figures of the Apostles. The central panels depict the Ascension, Resurrection, Assumption, and Nativity, while the other panels depict scenes from the life of Jesus and parts of the Old Testament. The *reja* makes it difficult to fully appreciate the paintings, but the sheer impact of the ensemble is unforgettable.

You exit the church under the curious wooden crocodile known as El Lagarto (the lizard), probably a replica of a gift from an Egyptian ruler wooing a Spanish infanta. The pretty Patio de los Naranjos is another Moorish original, formerly the ablutions courtyard of the mosque. It's shaded with the orange trees that give it its name. Admire the lofty Puerta de la Concepción (20th century, but faithful to the cathedral's style) before you exit through the Puerta del Perdón.

★ Real Alcázar

Plaza del Triunfo s/n, **T** 954 502 323, www.patronato-alcazar
sevilla.es *Tue-Sat 0930-1900, Sun 0930-1700, last entry 1 hr earlier.
€5, students free. A series of elaborately furnished chambers are visited
on the €3 guided tour, which leaves roughly half-hourly. Prebooking is
advisable,* **T** *954 560 040. The informative audio tour (Spanish, French,
English, German, Italian) is well-presented and makes good use of
quotes from the various kings responsible for the building's
construction. Bus 40, C3, C4.* Map 2, G4, p251

From the entry to the Alcázar through the dramatic Puerta del
León onwards, it's a pretty special place. While it's called the
Alcázar, and you'll see horseshoe arches, stucco, calligraphy, and
coffered ceilings throughout, it's not a Moorish palace. It used to
be, but little remains from that period; it owes its Moorish look to
the Castillian kings who built it, Alfonso X and his son Pedro I. As
well as being a sumptuous palace, the Alcázar was once a
considerable fortress in this impressively fortified city, a fact easily
appreciable as you pass through the chunky walls through the red
Puerta del León, named for the tiled king of beasts guarding it.
You emerge onto a large courtyard where the king's Hunt once
assembled. It's dominated by the impressive façade of the main
palace of the Castillian kings, built over the remains of two
previous Moorish palaces. Before heading into this, investigate
the Patio del Yeso to the left, one of the few remaining Moorish
structures, where lobed arches face horseshoe ones across a pool
surrounded by myrtle hedges. It's viewed from the Hall of Justice,
with stucco work and an octagonal coffered ceiling. Opposite,

> **!**
> **•** The king that built much of the Alcázar, Pedro I, was a
> curious character. One of his favourite pastimes was to
> dress in civilian clothes and prowl the streets of Seville by
> night, drinking in taverns and trying to get into fights so he
> could practise his swordsmanship.

across the courtyard, are chambers built by Fernando and Isabel to control New World affairs. Magellan planned his trip here and there's an important *retablo* from this period of the Virgen de los Navegantes. In the main panel by Alejo Fernández, the Virgin spreads her protective mantle over Columbus, Carlos V, as well as a shadowy group of indigenous figures. They might see trouble coming if they could glimpse the side panel of Santiago, Spain's patron, who is gleefully decapitating Moors.

From this main courtyard, if you arrive early, it is possible to see some of the upper floor of the palace, still used when Spanish royals are in town.

The façade of the palace is a curious mixture of Christian and Moorish styles that just about achieves superb harmony. Inscriptions about the glory of Allah – Pedro I was a pretty enlightened man – adjoin more conventional Latin ones proclaiming royal greatness.

This fusion of styles is repeated throughout the whole of this part of the palace, centred around the stunning Patio de las Doncellas, surprisingly reached by ducking down a small corridor. Throughout the complex are *azulejos*, topped by friezes of ceramic decoration, while higher up, intricate stucco friezes are surmounted by a range of marvellous inlaid ceilings. Applied colour is evident throughout, particularly on the inspired Puerta de los Pavones, named for the peacocks visible on it. The central patio had its upper gallery added by Carlos V, who also paved over Pedro I's Moorish garden. Part of this has recently been excavated, and debate over what to do with it is ongoing. Also worth admiring are the imposing doors, some incredibly elaborately inlaid. Among the rooms off this courtyard are the Salón de Embajadores, with a beautiful half-orange ceiling and a frieze of Spanish kings; and the chapel, where Charles V married his first cousin Isabella of Portugal (one of many inbreedings that doomed the line). To commemorate the event, he put in a wooden ceiling where elaborate mouldings are interspersed with busts.

High-rise living
Seville's gorgeous balconies provide Spanish sun spots to relax on.

Moving on from here is the Renaissance palace, heavily altered from the original Gothic by Carlos V and his descendants. In the chapel is an interesting Velásquez portraying a beautiful Virgin placing a chasuble over the shoulders of San Ildefonso. The two main chambers beyond here are decorated with tapestries.

From here stretches the vast and fantastic garden (top tip is to take a picnic, though don't make it super obvious at the entrance); different sections filled with slurping carp, palm trees, and a grotesque gallery built into a section of the old walls. It's TARDIS-like; difficult to envisage how such a large garden exists in the city centre. You finally exit the complex through the vestibule where the coaches and horses used to roll in and you emerge in the pretty Patio de Banderas.

Plaza Virgen de los Reyes
Bus no 40, C3, C4. Map 2, E4, p250

Filled with wooden seating in Semana Santa, as *sevillanos* watch the brotherhoods exit the cathedral, this little square is normally full of tourists craning their necks at the Giralda and horse carriages touting for a trot around the city. From here, Calle Mateos Gago rises, laden with tapas bars, into the Barrio Santa Cruz. A building that would turn heads anywhere except where it stands, under the shadow of the Giralda, the **Palacio Arzobispal** is an early 18th-century baroque masterpiece, unfortunately not open to the public (appointments are nominally on **T** 954 227 163, but you'd need a serious reason to get in). The red façade is gravely interspersed with white pilasters, while small iron awnings protect the upper windows from the fierce summer sun. The elaborate portal has ornate vegetal motifs and several escutcheons and is unusually topped by two vases of bronze flowers. The doors themselves are high and studded, with leonine knockers. Inside, you can see the main courtyard (beyond the smart archiepiscopal cars) with a pretty fountain and orange trees. This courtyard was once prowled by a lion cub, given to an archbishop by a solicitous duke; it was thought that burying feet afflicted by gout in the soft fur alleviated the condition. The cub was de-toothed and clawed but still managed to savage the horses of several of the prelate's visitors.

The adjacent square, **Plaza del Triunfo**, is up against the imposing walls of the Alcázar. It is centred around a monument dedicated to the Immaculate Virgin. The question as to whether Mary was conceived free of original sin was a subject for impassioned debate and even riots in the 17th century; the four famous *sevillanos* depicted here were all staunch advocates of her Immaculate-ness, and their view was eventually upheld by the Vatican.

● *From Plaza Virgen de los Reyes, go up the tiny alley behind the phone boxes opposite the archbishop's palace. You'll come to a tiny, tranquil cobbled square with a marble crucifix, pretty houses, and orange trees.*

★ Archivo de las Indias

Plaza del Triunfo s/n, **T** 954 211 234. Due to open in mid-2004.
Bus 40, C3, C4. Map 2, G3, p251

"An immense icebox of granite guarded by lions, in which is housed the colonial past, every sigh and every comma, until the end of the world." C. Nooteboom, *Roads to Santiago*

This square and sober Renaissance building offsets the cathedral and Alcázar on either side and was once Seville's Lonja, where merchants met to broker trade with the New World. The cannon poking out from the roof echo the decks of Spain's ocean-going vessels. In the late 18th century it was converted into the state archive, where all documents relating to the Americas were stored and filed. It's a unique and fascinating record of the discovery and administration of empire; from the excited scribblings of Columbus to the most mundane bookkeeping of remote jungle outposts. There are fascinating displays for the public, but the building is currently undergoing major renovation.

Avenida de la Constitución

Bus 40, C3, C4. Map 2, G3, p251

Once the city's major entrance point, busy Avenida de la Constitución flanks the cathedral's western façade. A small, Moorish tower is well-preserved at the corner of Calle Santo Tómas with blind lobed arches; there are many other interesting buildings, including the fabulous neo-Moorish confection of the Filella Confitería, which also does some excellent almond biscuits.

● *From Av de la Constitución, wander down a passage opposite the cathedral's western façade and you'll find yourself in a lovely semicircular space with a colonnade and peaceful fountain; the Plaza del Cabildo. It's lined with stamp and coin shops – you can also buy convent pastries here.*

Barrio Santa Cruz

*Once home to much of Seville's Jewish population, atmospheric Santa Cruz is the most charming of the city's barrios: a web of narrow, pedestrian lanes linking attractive small plazas with orange trees and shady terraces aplenty. Squeezed between the Alcázar, cathedral, and a section of the old city walls, it's heavily touristy but thankfully not over-prettified, and there's a fairly standard tourist beat that you can easily get away from. There are excellent accommodation and restaurant options as well as several intriguing antique and handicraft shops; even the souvenir shops are fairly tasteful. While there are a few sights of interest, such as the excellent baroque church of **Santa María la Blanca** and the **Hospital de los Venerables**, the main enjoyment to be had is wandering around and trying to guess where you'll end up.*

▸▸ *See Sleeping p113, Eating and drinking p128, Bars and clubs p149*

From the Plaza del Triunfo by the cathedral, head through the gate in the Alcázar walls to the south into the pretty square of Patio de Banderas, floored with sand and lined with orange trees. In the opposite corner duck through a small tunnel and twist your way onto Calle Judería, the most atmospheric way to enter and one of the nooks with the most mediaeval flavour. Bus 40, C3, C4

 Sights

Plazas de los Venerables, Alianza and Doña Elvira
Map 2, G5, p251

Although it's the most touristy part of the barrio, it's worth lingering a moment here to appreciate these three picturesque plazas, the latter shaded with orange trees. As well as several decent places to stay around here, there are many attractive

Remains of the day
The sun casts its long shadow on a whitewashed wall close to the bullring.

terraced eateries. Although you'll hear few Sevillian accents, the food at places like Casa Cueva or Bar Roman lives up to the barrio's atmosphere. In Plaza Alianza is the one-time studio of the late American painter and matador John Fulton, a fascinating all-round character who died in 1998.

Hospital de los Venerables

Plaza de los Venerables 8, **T** 954 562 696, www.focus.abengoa.es *Mon-Sun 1000-1400, 1600-2000. €4.75 . The price of admission includes a thorough, but slightly annoying, audio-guide which gives good information on the building and its contents (Spanish, English, German, with French to come soon).* Map 2, F5, p250

Built in the late-17th century in charitable vein, the "Venerables" refers to the old priests for whom it was originally intended as a hospital and residence. Now owned and run by a cultural foundation, the building holds frequent excellent temporary exhibitions on Sevillian culture and history, but is also worth visiting for its church, a repository for some fine painting of the late Sevillian school. The church lies along one side of the main courtyard, a noble space centred around a sunken fountain and surrounded by an arcade of marble columns. Stunning tilework completes the effect. Entering the church you are immediately struck by the frescoes on the walls, aisles, and vaulting; the first two by Lucas Valdés, the latter by his father Juan de Valdés Leal, who also painted the fine ceiling fresco in the sacristy depicting angels carrying the cross.Several *retablos* line the walls, two with balconies inbuilt so that old priests who couldn't make it down the stairs could still attend Mass. Worth noting are two lustrous panels painted onto copper by an anonymous Flemish artist and Lucas Valdés' Last Supper in the later (19th century) main *retablo*. By the door are two Pedro Roldán sculptures of San Fernando, sword in hand, and St Peter; the church is dedicated to these two.

★ **Tiled murals**

Best

• The Studebaker ad on C Tetuán
• The *manzanilla* ad on C Pavia in El Arenal
• The Torre del Oro in an alley off C Cuna, opposite C Cerrajería
• The forge on the façade of number 94, C Rodrigo de Triana
• The river and docks in the portal of C Mateos Gago 39

Murallas Almohades
C Agua s/n. *Map 2, G6, p251*

The Barrio de Santa Cruz is still hemmed in by a long stretch of the Moorish city walls, on the other side of which stand the Jardines de Murillo. A couple of the watchtowers are still in place. These, which once numbered 166, contributed to the city's imposing defences; Seville's walls had a circumference of some six kilometres and it was known as one of the most heavily fortified cities in Europe. Jump on bus C4 to give you an idea of exactly how big they were; its circular route almost exactly follows their original perimeter.

Jardines de Murillo
Summer 0800-2400, winter 0800-2200. Bus no C3, C4.
Map 2, G7, p251

Beyond the walls stands this narrow public park, with its elegant paths and collection of interesting trees, including several palms and a eucalyptus that's pushing 40 m. The space was given to the city by King Alfonso XIII as part of the preparations for the 1929 Ibero-American Exhibition and is centred around a monument to Columbus. A lion stands atop a double column; a ship sails awkwardly halfway up, and on either side are commemorated the names of Fernando and Isabel, the monarchs who sent Columbus forth. In the top (northern) corner of the gardens is a small symbol of the *Reconquista* – one of the Moorish towers was incorporated into a Christian palace and has been emblazoned with a knightly shield.

Calle Santa María la Blanca
Bus C3, C4. Map 2, E7, p250

This street was once one of the city's entrances, entering the walls at the Puerta de la Carne, named because the food markets used to be in this zone and farmers would enter here with carts piled with meat, cereals and vegetables. These days, it's more of a plaza than a street, with several sun-kissed terraces attracting tourists (go for *Carmela* or *Altamira* ahead of any place with plastic paellas on display). Try and be here around 1830, for then you can nip into the small church of the same name when it opens just before Mass starts. The attractive, toothed arch of the portal gives little hint of the baroque fantasy inside – the central vault of the triple-naved church is carved with a riot of floral and vegetal decoration, an astounding sight. There's a small, similarly decorated cupola with an image of the Giralda, while the Virgin, dressed in white, takes pride of place in the golden *retablo*. Look left and you'll see a Murillo; a Last Supper scene that's not counted among his finest works but certainly deserves to be. A young, visionary Christ is surrounded by the wise, bearded old heads of his apostles; it's all the better for being in situ.

● *After having an outdoor tapa and beer in the street, leave it on Calle Ximénez de Enciso. Just around the corner, in No 30, a red house, there's a beautiful patio, tiled foyer, and carved portal. It's usually open, but peek don't pry; it's private property.*

!
● Painter John Fulton saw his first bullfight at 20 and became the first American to become a full Spanish matador. Juan Belmonte described him as the best non-Latin he had ever seen in the ring and his art is equally highly regarded.

Casa de la Memoria de Al-Andalus

C Ximénez de Enciso 28, **T** 954 560 670, memorias@teleline.es
Mon-Sun 0900-1400, 1800-2000. €1 (free with show ticket).
Map 2, E6, p250

This house has been beautifully done up as a venue for high-quality flamenco as well as other performances of Muslim and Jewish inspiration (see Entertainment, p166). There's also a small exhibition with reproductions of Moorish and Jewish instruments and ceramics, and a not-entirely-accurate wistful perspective on the tolerance of Muslim rule in Andalucía.

Casa-Museo de Murillo

C Santa Teresa 8. *Mon-Fri 1000-1330, 1600-1830. Free.*
Map 2, F6, p250

You can see the ground floor, where there's a patio, scarce biographical notes, and a small inventory of Murillo's paintings in Seville. There's also a bookshop. Murillo's ashes were interred in a monastery church opposite. This was demolished in the 19th century; a small plaque around the corner on Plaza Santa Cruz has been erected in remembrance by the Academía de Bellas Artes, which Murillo founded in the 17th century.

★ Calle Mateos Gago

Map 2, E5, p250

Despite its tourist-central location, leading from the Giralda into the heart of Barrio Santa Cruz, this is one of Seville's best tapas streets. It takes at least four hours to fully appreciate its attractions and you'll likely be neither hungry nor sober by the end of it. There are plenty of tempting terraces too, but bear in mind that most bars only serve tapas-sized portions at the bar itself.

The tapas options dry up after Calle Mesón del Moro, but beyond here are two interesting plaques. One, opposite the *Hostal Goya* at the entrance to a school, sternly warns children to respect the lives and nests of birds (originally placed here in 1896 when a law made bird's-nesting illegal). At the end of the street, another inscription commemorates the birthplace of Cardinal Wiseman, the most influential figure in the revival of Roman Catholicism in Britain in the mid-19th century. His much acclaimed anecdotal novel, *Fabiola*, was named after the street the house stands on.

Plaza Alfalfa
Bus no 10, 32. Map 2, B5, p250

All roads lead to Plaza Alfalfa, but not if you're actually looking for it; it's tucked away in the tortuous lanes in the north of the barrio, near Plaza del Salvador. Formerly an animal-feed market (alfalfa is lucerne), the stalls still go up on a Sunday morning, although this time they're selling animals themselves, from caged birds to puppies to something straight for the pot. The square is busy day and night, first with café action, then with some no-frills but quality tapas, and later with a high concentration of late-opening bars.

South of the cathedral

Much of the area south of the cathedral is taken up with the large **Parque María Luisa**, *donated to the city by the queen's sister in the late 19th century. It was used as the site for the grandiose 1929 Ibero-American Exhibition, an event on a massive scale that the dictatorship hoped would re-establish Seville and Spain in the world spotlight. The legacy of the exhibition is a public park and a beautiful series of buildings that were the pavilions. The* **Plaza de España** *is an impressive space and the* **Hotel Alfonso XIII** *one of the most sumptuous in Spain. Two of the pavilions have been converted into outstanding museums and the whole area is much used for relaxing* *walks and picnics. It is also used by the university, whose main building is the massive old tobacco factory, second largest building in Spain and workplace of the fictional Carmen. A walk through this part of town provides a green break from urban Seville and a fascinating architectural ensemble from a period where lavish spending and blind optimism created buildings of astonishing cost and significant beauty just years away from a civil war that plunged the city and country into decades of poverty and monoculturalism.*

▸▸ *See Sleeping p117, Eating and drinking p131, Bars and clubs p150*

Sights

Hotel Alfonso XIII

C San Fernando 2, **T** 954 917 000, www.hotel-alfonsoxiii.com
Bus C3, C4, 40. Map 2, I3, p251

This massive and elegant neo-Moorish hotel was built for the 1929 exhibition to put up the important visitors. It's an indication of how grandiose a project the show was; seemingly every inch is tiled or marbled, and the furniture lacks little by comparison. The public can wander in to the central patio with its fountain or have a drink in the bar; it's worth a look at the opulence that has made it one of Spain's most famous hotels. See also Sleeping, p117.

Antigua Fábrica de Tabacos

C San Fernando 4, **T** 954 551 000. *Mon-Fri 0800-2030. Free.*
Bus C1, C2, C3, C4. Map 2, J4, p251

Visitors flocked to the cigarette factory in the late 19th century to see the girls at work, for it had been made famous by Carmen and other tales of the beauty of Seville's womenfolk. It's a massive building, Spain's second-largest, and is surrounded by a fence and moat; tight security once aimed at stopping the workers nicking fags. Despite poor conditions, the workers can have had no complaints about the building itself, with numerous elegant hallways and courtyards that suit it perfectly to its new function as a university building. It's a lively place to wander around; the crescendo of noise increases as you approach the centre of the matrix of corridors, and the lingering cigarette smoke adds an authentic touch.

Palacio de San Telmo

Av de Roma s/n, **T** 954 597 505. *Visits only by prior appointment. Free. Bus C3, C4, 40. Map 2, J3, p251*

This elegant building is very typical of Sevillian baroque, red and yellow ochre in colour and built in the 17th and 18th centuries to train sea captains. It was chosen as a palace by Infanta María Luisa, sister of Isabel II, and her husband, the Duc de Montpensier before being given to the city in the late 19th century. It's now the office of the premier of Andalucía and access to the interior depends if there's a visit arranged; call and find out. Otherwise, admire the main façade, which is ornate without being kitsch. The columns are carved with mythical scenes and are topped by a pretty balcony.

The 1929 Pavilions

Bus: C1, C2. Map 2, L5, p251

Around this area are the majority of the pavilions built for the 1929 Ibero-American Exhibition. Mostly in use, they are fun to wander around. One has been converted into a *discoteca*, many are in use by the university, while the attractive Peruvian pavilion is the headquarters of the Parque Nacional Coto Doñana. The Teatro Lope de Vega is a lovely art nouveau/deco fusion among it all, while there are a few more worth checking out at the other end of Parque María Luisa, such as the Colombian (now the consulate)

★ **Peaceful terraces**

- Capote, a corner of a Cuban beach by the Guadalquivir, p153
- Esfera, a café in the old Expo site, p142
- La Huerta de la Buhaira, a lovely spot in a park, p144
- Kiosko del Agua, an excellent riverside spot, p150
- Chile, a little place among the old exhibition buildings, p132

and Moroccan pavilions. The small tourist office on the roundabout predates the exhibition; it was once the gatehouse for the Palacio de San Telmo but was later made famous as the sewing room of the consumptive daughter of María Luisa, who married her first cousin Alfonso XII for love but died six months later in 1878.

Plaza de España
Bus C1, C2. Map 2, L7, p251

This huge space was the pièce de resistance of the 1929 exhibition. Designed and planned as far back as 1913 by Aníbal González, the event's master-architect, it was envisaged as a 'second Giralda', a symbol of a new dynamic Seville. The semicircular area is backed by a massive brick and marble building that curves around to two proud towers. A small canal was once used for leisurely rowing and is crossed by four bridges. It's a popular spot at weekends, and despite being a little careworn and pigeon-soiled, it's a good place to hang out. The most endearing feature is the row of benches, each one dedicated to one of Spain's provinces. The buildings are used now for various goverment departments, but it's no surprise that the stunning ensemble has been used in several films, including Lawrence of Arabia, and, most recently, *Star Wars: The Attack of the Clones*.

★ Parque María Luisa
Daily 0800-2400 summer, 2200 winter. Free.
Bus C1, C2, 30, 31, 33, 34. Map 2, L6, p251

This beautiful and peaceful space is Seville's nicest park, again developed for the 1929 exhibition. It's full of quiet corners, even on busy days, and a series of informative plaques detail the huge range of exotic trees and plants on show; parts of the park even feel like an authentic rainforest. Among the paths are numerous *glorietas* (little clearings) dedicated to famous Sevillian figures. There's cycle hire available, as well as plenty of horse carriages to clop you around. There are also decent watering holes at each end, Citroën by the Plaza de España and Bilindo by the Plaza de América; both have a good terrace and do tasty tapas.

Monument to Bécquer
Parque de María Luisa s/n. *Bus C1, C2. Map 2, L6, p251*

The most famous of the park's *glorietas* is near the Plaza de España and dedicated to the romantic poet Gustavo Adolfo Bécquer (1836-1870). His poems centred around love, frequently unrequited or anguished; he died at the age of 34 of pneumonia-related illnesses. The beautiful memorial is built around a tree and is often adorned with fresh flowers; his work is much loved in Spain. The three girls represent the stages of love (love found, in love, love lost) while behind them lies a fallen Eros with a dagger in his side.

! The Parque María Luisa's neo-Moorish lines have become any number of exotic cities on the silver screen from Cairo and Damascus in *Lawrence of Arabia* to Tangiers in *The Wind and the Lion* and even in a galaxy far far away in *Star Wars – The Attack of the Clones.*

Museo de Artes y Costumbres Populares de Sevilla
Pl de América 3, **T** 954 232 576, www.juntadeandalucia.es/
cultura *Tue 1500-2000, Wed-Sat 0900-2000, Sun 0900-1400.*
Free for EU citizens, €1.50 others. Explanations in Spanish only.
Bus 30, 31, 33, 34. Map 1, L5, p249

In the rather majestic (if a little decayed at the back) Mudéjar
pavilion from the exhibition is an excellent museum, a cut above
the dreary displays that this type of subject seems to produce all
too often. The top floor is mostly devoted to what Sevillians wore
through the centuries; there's a good blend of period paintings
and costumes themselves. In the massive basement there are
many items of furniture and household use as well as
reconstructions of typical workshops, including a guitar
makers and a wine *bodega* whose smell permeates the level.

★ **Museo Arqueológico**
Pabellón de Bellas Artes, Pl de América s/n, **T** 954 232 401,
www.juntadeandalucia.es/cultura *Tue 1400-2000, Wed-Sat
0900-2000, Sun 0900-1430, free for EU, €1.50 otherwise. There are
English summaries at the entrance to most rooms and a decent
printed handout/guide. Bus 30, 31, 33, 34.* Map 1, L6, p249

Seville's archaeological museum should be good, considering the
wealth of people that have lived and traded in the region since
prehistoric times. And it doesn't disappoint, with a rich Roman
collection that holds its own for quality against Europe's finest.
Among a good selection of prehistoric finds and fossils the
standout pieces are from the mysterious Tartessian culture; a
people that lived in the Guadalquivir valley from about 1100 BC
on. Their finest pieces, finely worked pottery, carved stone, and
gold jewellery show clear influences from the Phoenicians, who
began trading along this coast some time around 700 BC. Their
principal goddess, Astarte, is represented in a good bronze. On

the ground floor, after an imposing array of Iberian stone lions, come the Roman finds, mostly from nearby Itálica, but many also from the large necropolis at Carmona (see p97 and p100).

There are several mosaics; one from Ecija depicting Bacchus and his leashed leopards, and a later one showing the Judgement of Paris with Aphrodite seemingly keen to win the contest. Among the excellent sculptures on display are a 2nd century AD headless Venus, striding out of the waves at the moment of her birth, a slightly later Diana, the emperor Trajan in full heroic mould, and an excellent likeness of the bearded Hadrian. There's a collection of citizens' portrait heads – a real rogues' gallery – and a fascinating room full of bronze law scrolls. A curious ensemble of carved footprints rounds off an excellent collection.

● *Turn right out of the museum and straight across Avenida de la Borbolla up Calle Felipe II. This is the well-heeled residential district of El Porvenir. Few tourists make it here, but ask anyone around here what the city's best tapas bar is, and they'll say* Joaquín Márquez, *at number 8 on this street, for its excellent blend of the traditional and the innovative. There are several others around this area too.*

El Arenal

If you look at a picture of Seville in the early 19th century or earlier, you'll see that from the Moorish **Torre del Ore** *the city wall recedes from the riverbank, leaving a large open area, El Arenal. This was a haunt of thieves, swindlers, prostitutes, and smugglers, who liked to hang out near the docks, where the action was. Built up in the 19th century, El Arenal is now one of Seville's most pleasant barrios, with some of its major landmarks and the moving art of the* **Hospital de Caridad.** *The* **Río Guadalquivir** *itself is a major attraction here; although there are no longer galleons bound for the Spanish Main, there are several outdoor bars, river cruises, and a place to hire canoes. The Arenal has a wealth of excellent tapas bars worth extensive exploration. It's also the home of bullfighting in Seville*

with the elegant Maestranza wedged into a city block on the river-
front; it's one of Spain's principal temples of the activity. The attractive
modern Teatro de la Maestranza echoes the bullring's shape.

▸▸ *See Sleeping p117, Eating and drinking p132, Bars and clubs p150*

◉ Sights

Torre del Oro
Paseo de Colón s/n, **T** 954 222 419. *Tue-Fri 1000-1400, Sat-Sun*
1100-1400. €1. Bus C3, C4, 40. Map 2, J1, p251

The spiky battlements of this beautiful Moorish tower are one
of Seville's primary landmarks and the building is powerfully
evocative of the city's military and maritime history. Located at
a pivotal point of the town's walls, on the river, its duty was to
prevent landings in the Arenal area and damage to the docks,
and to protect the unwalled Triana bank. To this end, a heavy
chain was sometimes stretched across the river, an effective
but ultimately futile tactic. The exterior was once decorated
with bright, golden ceramic tiles, from which it gets its name.

The interior now holds a motley maritime museum with sharks'
teeth, and paintings of galleons and sea dogs unilluminated by any
explanatory panels. It's worth going in, however, for the old prints
showing Seville in the late 16th century. The Arenal is the sandy
thieves' haunt it once was, Triana has its boat-bridge and castle,
and the docks are bristling with boats.

● *Directly opposite the Torre del Oro, head through a passage in the*
large insurance building and round the corner to another pretty and
well-preserved Almohad tower, named the Torre de Plata. Then head
through another passageway further around the insurance building
for another view of it, as well as a section of the old city walls.

La Maestranza

Paseo de Colón 12, **T** 954 224 577, www.realmaestranza.com
Mon-Sun 0930-1400, 1500-1900 except fight days (spring and
summer Sun and all week during Feria), when it's open 0930-1500,
guided tours every 30 mins (English and Spanish).€4. Bus C4.
Map 3, E8, p252

One of Spain's temples of bullfighting, La Maestranza is a beautiful
building wedged into a city block, which accounts for its slightly
elliptical shape. Started in the mid-18th century, it took until the
late 19th century to finish it. It holds some 14,000 spectators and
sells out nearly every seat during the April Feria when the most
prestigious fights of the season are held. The Seville crowd are
among the most knowledgeable of *aficionados*, and many of
bullfighting's most famous names have been *sevillanos* (see box
p59). See a fight here if you can; the guided tour is a poor
substitute for the atmosphere at the *corridas*. The tour is brisk and
not especially informative unless you know something about the
sport; if you want to learn how a bullfight works, you won't learn
it here (the Carmen tour, see p29, actually has more of this sort of
information). The tour takes you through the main entrance, the
Puerta del Príncipe, which has an imposing wrought-iron gateway
by Pedro Roldán; it's a 16th-century work that originally stood in a
convent. If a *torero* has a particularly good day, he is carried out
through this door. The tour also takes in the small museum, which
has some good pictures of the chaotic affairs that were early
bullfights before the present structure of a fight was adopted in
1830. There are paintings of famous fighters and heads of famous
bulls. You also briefly visit the horse stables, but disappointingly
not the bullpens. Nor are you permitted onto the sand itself
(usually the biggest thrill of a bullring visit). You do, however, see
the small chapel where bullfighters can pray before the fight. It's
dedicated to the Virgen de la Caridad, patron of bullfighters.
Another favoured Virgin is La Macarena, and it's her who appears

▶ Bullfighting's Golden Age

Seville has always produced more than its share of great bullfighters, but none perhaps will ever touch the heights of two contemporaries, Juan Belmonte and Joselito "El Gallo".

Belmonte was a perfectionist who completely changed bullfighting with his technical perfection and inch-perfect positioning. "The way Belmonte worked was not a heritage, nor a development, it was a revolution", said Ernest Hemingway of his utterly novel approach. By contrast, Joselito, a young gypsy from a bullfighting family, was an artist, wholly elegant, all instinct and grace, and completely without fear. The rivalry between the two took bullfighting to new heights and the period is known as the Golden Age.

Joselito was only just 25 when he was fatally gored in the act of killing a bull in Talavera. The nation was shocked, as he had seemed untouchable. Belmonte survived bullfighting and became a bull breeder himself before shooting himself in 1962, months after applauding his friend Hemingway's identical action. Both their tombs can be seen at the Seville cemetery (see p84).

above the door to the Infirmary, a chillingly modern room where horn wounds are operated on. The Macarena seems to be doing a good job; no bullfighter has died in the ring in Spain since 1984.

Outside the bullring are three statues; alongside is the much-loved Curro Romero, a recently retired matador, while opposite is Pepe Luís Vásquez, another bullfighter, and, of course, the fictional Carmen, heroine of the story by Mérimée and the opera by Bizet. Her betrothed was so jealous of her love for a bullfighter here that he took her life.

Teatro de la Maestranza

Paseo Colón 22, **T** 954 226 573, www.teatromaestranza.com
Bus C4. *Map 2, H1, p251*

Designed for the 1992 Expo by Aurelio del Pozo and Luís Marín de Teran, this theatre incorporates an older façade and echoes the shape of the nearby bullring of the same name. It's an attractive, modern building with a fairly steely exterior and a softer more elegant interior. It hosts a range of ballet, opera, and drama in its two theatres, but is not open to the public at other times.

★ Hospital de la Caridad

C Temprado 3, **T** 954 223 232. *Mon-Sat 0900-1330, 1530-1830, Sun 0900-1300. €3. Bus C4.* *Map 2, G2, p251*

Behind the theatre is this *residencia de ancianos* (nursing home) still fulfilling its original charitable purpose. It was built as a hospital for the poor by Miguel de Mañara, a curious 17th-century *sevillano* often likened to Don Juan. After a scandalous youth of seduction and deceit he reformed completely after seeing a vision of his own death and dedicated himself to a life of charity and religion. He had a good eye for art; as a result of this, the hospital chapel has a collection of masterpieces by Sevillan masters. The façade of the hospital is in attractively sober Seville style in contrast to the chapel, which is beautifully decorated with blue and white *azulejos*. Astride horses, St George and St James kill dragon and Moors respectively, while the virtues Faith, Charity, and Hope are represented in other panels. Faith and Charity are represented in the pretty double patio too, as the centrepiece of the fountains.

    The church's artwork was commissioned by Mañara expressly to remind his brotherhood of the charitable virtues and the futility of wordly wealth and pride. Two astonishing paintings stand above and opposite the entrance. They are the two finest, and most disturbing, works of the Seville painter Juan de Valdés Leal. The first one you'll see depicts a leering skeletal Death with a scythe, putting out a candle with one hand while trampling over objects that represent wordly wealth, power, and knowledge. The inscription 'In Ictu Oculi' translates as 'in the blink of an eye'. Opposite this is an even more challenging painting entitled *Finis Gloriae Mundi* ('the end of wordly glory'). It depicts a crypt in which a dead bishop and knight are being eaten by worms. Above, a balance is borne by the hand of Christ. On one side are symbols of the seven deadly sins, on the other side symbols of a holy love of God and Christ. "Neither more nor less" read the words on the scales. Mañara commissioned these works very exactly, and the face of the knight is thought to be his own.

After these grim warnings, the paintings of Murillo demonstrate the charitable life Mañara wanted his brotherhood to lead. Although four are missing (they were stolen by Napoleon's pillaging general, Soult and are now scattered around the world; they include the impressive Return of the Prodigal Son in Washington) those that remain are exceptional examples of this artist's work. St John of God carries a sick man, while St Isabelle of Hungary cares for the afflicted. A Moses horned with light brings forth water from the rock, while Jesus feeds the multitude with loaves and fishes. In a *retablo* by Bernardo Simón de Pineda next to the pulpit is another Murillo painting, an Annunciation. The pulpit is another symbolic work; atop it is Roldán's Charity, while at the base of the stairs is a wooden depiction of evil vanquished. Roldán is also responsible for the figures in the intense *retablo* of Santo Cristo de la Caridad, with a Christ dripping blood flanked by cherubs.

!
•
Margarita Carmen Dolores Cansino, better known as Rita Hayworth, was born in New York of a Sevillian father, Eduardo. Her second husband Orson Welles also had a Seville connection – he spent some time in the city writing articles and learning to fight bulls, without much success.

Horsing around
An elegantly dressed horse and his carriage are a common sight in central Seville .

Juan de Valdés Leal painted the ceiling, of which the cupola is particularly fine, while Murillo also painted the small panels of the infants Jesus and John the Baptist above two other *retablos*. The main *retablo*, a Churrigueresque riot of cherubs and *solomónica* columns, is again the work of Roldán and Pineda; the former responsible for the emotive central tableau of the burial of Christ. Mortuus et sepultus est reads the inscription; the curiously misplaced grandfather clock alongside is a feature of many Seville churches. The gallery is dignified by another good Valdés Leal work, the Exaltation of the Cross.

Triana

Triana is many people's favourite part of Seville. It's redolent with history from every epoch of the Christian city as well as having a picturesque riverfront lined with terraced bars and restaurants. It was for a long time the gypsy barrio and as such the home of flamenco in Seville. Although most of the gypsies were moved on in the 1950s, its backstreet bars are still the best place to catch impromptu performances. Triana is also famous for ceramics; most of the azulejo tiles that so beautifully decorate Seville's houses come from here, and there are still many workshops in the area. It's also got a significant maritime history; many of the streets are named after sailors that undertook voyages to the New World; Triana has a namesake in Las Palmas for this reason. The now-disappeared castle of San Jorge was a major centre of the Spanish Inquisition and the working-class district was the seat of early resistance to the military coup of 1936; as such, much of the barrio was destroyed by the army in the early days of the Civil War. It's got a different feel to the rest of the city, and trianeros are still a tight-knit social group. Many residents once lived in corrales de vecinos, houses centred around a common courtyard; there are still a few around. Look out too for the many azulejo plaques dedicated to flamenco singers and important people in the religious cofradías while wandering around, and be sure not to miss some of the city's most revered religious images, such as the sublime El Cachorro, or the Esperanza de Triana, the most-loved Virgin after La Macarena. While the riverfront and surrounds are fairly trendy these days, venture into some of the smaller backstreets and you'll find that Triana preserves more of its history and associations than any other part of Seville.

▸▸ *See Sleeping p118, Eating and drinking p135, Bars and clubs p150*

Sights

Puente de Triana
Bus C4, 43. Map 3, F5, p252

The best way to approach Triana is across the Puente Isabel II, usually simply called Puente de Triana. Amazingly for a city with such an important history, this was the first proper bridge it had; opened in 1852, it replaced a dicey affair built on boats tied together. In fact, some historians cite the lack of a previous bridge as an important factor in Seville's decline, or at least of the attitude that partly caused it. At night you'll get fantastic views of Triana's waterfront and the floodlit Torre del Oro from here. At the bridge's southern end is a small chapel and the Faro de Triana restaurant. The bridge ends in Plaza Altozano with a lively market building and two statues. One is dedicated to flamenco and depicts a singer with a guitar and her foot on an anvil, traditional accompaniment to *martinetes* (an early flamenco form). The other statue is the proud figure of Juan Belmonte, who vies with his contemporary and fellow *sevillano* Joselito El Gallo for the title of the greatest bullfighter ever (see box p59). Though he survived death on the horns, life away from the ring was never happy. Hearing of his friend Ernest Hemingway's suicide, he replied "Well done", and did the same five months later.

★ Calle Betis
Bus C3, 40. Map 3, I7, p253

Betis was the name of the Río Guadalquivir in pre-Moorish days and this street runs along its Triana bank. It's one of the top strolls in the city lined with prettily coloured houses. There's something here for everyone, whether downing finely-textured seafood on an outdoor terrace, snacking on tasty grilled sardines at *Los Chorritos*, or drinking and dancing until all hours in any number of places along the strip.

Bridge with a view
Walkway to Triana over Puente Isabel II.

Iglesia de Santa Ana

C Pureza s/n. *Mon-Sun 0900-1100, 1900-2100 (depending on restoration works). Free. Map 3, I7, p253*

The 'Cathedral of Triana' is believed to be Seville's oldest church, dating from around 1276. It was founded by Alfonso X of Castilla, the arms of which can still be seen above the attractive Gothic north door, with a fine archivolt. The bright tower, yellow with blue ceramic stripes, is a later addition. The interior is high, with three long brick-built naves. There are several items of interest, including a large silver monstrance and a charmingly tiled tomb. The highlight, however, is the *retablo*, in need of some cleaning, but an inspired work of painted panels by Pedro de Campaña centred around the Virgin with Santa Ana. The church is held in much esteem by *trianeros* and is a popular wedding spot.

Feria de Abril

Seville's April fiesta is a lively counterpoint to the solemnity of Semana Santa. Originating as a gypsy horse fair, it took its present form in the early 20th century. At last count the grounds in Los Remedios were home to 1,046 *casetas*.

The *casetas* are striped tents which become the venue for six days of socializing, eating, drinking and dancing. Most are privately owned bar a few public ones and entry is by invitation only. It's busy throughout; during the afternoon Sevillians dashingly dressed in horseman's suits and bright flamenca costumes parade in colourful carriages pulled by horses and mules, while the dancing and drinking action hots up at night. A large funfair adds to the attraction, while in the afterznoons the season's biggest bullfights are held at the Maestranza.

Getting there: The massive Feria gate is at the bottom of C Asunción, a 15-minute walk from the Puente de San Telmo.

Shuttle buses run from Prado San Sebastián station. Cars are not allowed near the grounds. Taxis are, but to get home you're much better walking, as the queues are horrendous. Otherwise, use the rank at the back exit rather than by the gate.

Kick-off: Feria begins on the Monday night two weeks after Easter Sunday (unless this would mean that it began in May, in which case it's brought forward). Crowds wait until midnight when the gate is spectacularly lit up and the party begins. It runs until the next Sunday when a fireworks display ends the revelry at midnight.

Casetas: Grab a map from tourist information; most of the public *casetas* are clearly marked; these belong to leftist political parties and the local city councils. If you know a local that can invite you in to a *caseta*, well and good, but it's fairly easy to get in to some of the less exclusive ones. Dress respectably and ask the doorman politely in Spanish if you can enter; you'll get plenty of knockbacks but also plenty of entries, particularly if a girl does the asking. Large groups of people speaking English will get nowhere. Up until about 2100, there are no doormen, and most *casetas* can be entered freely.

Eating and drinking: The best places to eat are the *casetas* themselves, which put on a range of tapas and *raciones*. Drink *manzanilla* (usually served in a half bottle) or *rebujito*, a weak, refreshing blend of the same with lemonade, served in a litre cup. *Pescaito frito* (fried fish) is eaten on the first night.

Toilets: Toilet queues in the public *casetas* are very long, so you're better going in a private one or paying €1 to use one of the few public loos around.

Sevillanas: "Sevillanas are the woman's chance to play a man like a *torero* plays a bull. If you dance with someone who knows what they're doing, it's incredibly intense; it's like making love" Inma Domínguez, *sevillana* dance teacher.

In all the *casetas*, once eating's done, people spend the night dancing. The *sevillana* is a relatively modern form with roots in both flamenco and Latin music. A dance has four distinct parts, all characterized by elaborate arms-aloft movements, partners stepping around each other, and stares of moody intensity. You'll experience another dimension of Feria if you manage to learn the basics.

Time-out: If you want a short break, head to C Virgen de las Montañas where La Guita is a large and good-value tapas bar with a large, covered terrace. You can get a seat, rest those legs, and eat and drink in comparative peace and quiet.

Kicking on: Unless you've hit a manic *caseta*, Feria winds down about 0300. If you want more, the best places are around the grounds on and near C Asunción; the rest of Seville's nightlife is comparatively quiet. Feria's biggest night is usually the Friday; Saturday isn't nearly as big.

La Esperanza de Triana

C Pureza 53. *Free. Map 3, I7, p253*

Behind the big yellow and white façade of the Capilla de los
Marineros lives La Esperanza de Triana. She and La Macarena are
the two most-adored Virgins of the city and there are few bars
around without a picture up of one or the other of them. They are
appropriately both named 'hope'; a necessary commodity in the past
for the inhabitants of Seville's two poorest barrios. Like La Macarena,
she is weeping and expensively clothed and wears a golden halo.
Her passages across the bridges in the wee hours of Good Friday
morning are among the most emotional of the Easter processions.

Calle de Castilla and around

Bus C3, 40. Map 3, E3, p252

Heading the other way from Puente de Triana will take you into the
lesser-known northern streets. Calle de Castilla is the principal one,
an interesting stroll enlivened by shops selling ceramics and
flamenco dresses. Just off Calle de Castilla, the Callejón de la
Inquisición is a spooky lane that used to lead from the river to the
Castillo San Jorge, the seat of the Inquisition – many a suspected
heretic or Jew climbed this way and bid goodbye to life. At 39 is
Nuestra Señora de la O with a dusky red tower topped in blue
and white ceramics and home to a revered statue of Mary.

● *Parallel is the street Alfarería named for its potteries. While most
of the ceramics shops don't make the produce on site, some do; poke
your head into no 22 and you might well see the old potter at work.*

! The Seville orange comes into season in early January and
● stays on the trees about a month. Don't try snacking on
them as their sharp, sour flavour appeals to few. However,
they make the best bitter marmalade – nearly all Andalucía's
crop goes into British jam jars.

Capilla de Patrocinio

C Castilla 182. *Mon-Sat 1030-1330, 1800-2130. Free.*
Bus C1/C2, C3, 40. Map 3, D1, p252

This unremarkable building is decorated with blue tiles narrating the story of the life of Mary and the death and resurrection of Christ. It's worth a visit for the superb Christ figure inside, who is much revered across Seville. He is named El Cachorro, after a dead young gypsy that the sculptor is said to have used as a model. The sculpture is breathtaking; you can feel the sinews of the crucified Christ straining, while his face is a perfectly rendered mixture of anguish and relief.

Museo de Carruajes

Plaza de Cuba s/n, **T** 954 272 604, www.museodecarruajes.com
Fri-Sun 1100-1400. €3.60. Bus C3, 40. Map 2, K7, p251

If you're not here during Feria de Abril, this is the place to come to see a selection of the lovely horse carriages that are de rigueur for smart families at that time. Horses play a bigger part in the lives of many *sevillanos* than is common in the western world these days, and this likeable museum imparts some of that. It's set in a pretty old building just on the Los Remedios side of the Plaza de Cuba. Beyond here stretches the extensive barrio of Los Remedios, a fairly wealthy place these days, with streets of smart shops and some good lurking tapas options.

● *Turn right out of the museum and right along the riverbank. You'll soon reach a plaque which marks the point from where Magellan set sail in 1519 with a fleet of ships. He was aiming to sail around the world; he didn't make it, but some of his crewmen did, under Juan Sebastian Elkano, a Basque whom the street is named after.*

Centro and San Vicente

*Centro is at the centre of the old walled town and is the social hub of Seville life, at least during daylight hours. It's where people meet for a coffee, a business lunch, an evening paseo or a day's shopping. As such, it's replete with fine shops and civic plazas, as well as churches which aren't on the tourist circuit but feature stunning altarpieces or little-known masterpieces. The beautiful **Casa de Pilatos** should not be missed for its excellent patio and collection of classical sculpture and renaissance furnishings. Although there are only a couple of visiting slots per week, definitely try and schedule in a visit to the **Ayuntamiento**, whose interior more than matches the ornate Plateresque stonework of its rear façade. The adjacent barrio of San Vicente is a quieter zone centred around the not-to-be-bypassed Museo de Bellas Artes, Seville's main art gallery and a treasure trove of painting from the city's Golden Age. The district is mainly residential, but offers peaceful strolls around its attractive streets, many good accommodation options, particularly at the budget end, and a selection of cheerful, local bars.*

▸▸ *See Sleeping p118, Eating and drinking p138, Bars and clubs, p153*

 Sights

★ Casa de Pilatos

Plaza de Pilatos s/n, **T** *954 225 298. Mon-Sun 0900-1900.*
€5 lower floor, €8 both floors, free Tue from 1300.
Bus C1-C4 to Plaza San Agustín. Map 2, B7, p250

This stunning mansion is still partly inhabited by members of the family of the Dukes of Medinaceli, who built most of it in the late 15th century to early 16th century. It owes its name to the story that the Duke, on a pilgrimage to Jerusalem, was so struck by the former residence of the Roman governors (including Pontius

Pilate) that he decided to model his own house on it. The profusion of classical sculpture decorating the courtyards and gardens, some of it original, certainly gives the house a Roman air, but the architecture is principally a very attractive blend of Renaissance classicism and Mudéjar styles. Sensitive restoration has healed the damage caused during the Spanish Civil War when the building was used as a hospital.

The highlight of the visit is the central courtyard, reached from the entrance by passing under a thriving purple cascade of bougainvillea. It's a stunning combination of *azulejos* and stuccowork; the Italianate central fountain is overseen by statues, including an excellent Athena Promachos. On the walls are mounted a series of excellent Roman portrait heads, obtained by the Dukes from Italy, large chunks of which were under Aragonese control. More statues, some 16th century, decorate the rooms around, which feature further tile and plasterwork. The gardens are beautiful and peaceful; one even has a small grotto with tinkling water.

The staircase to the upper level is a cascade of shining tiles topped by a majestic golden dome that owes some of its decoration to Moorish mocárabes. Beyond here is accessed by a guided tour, *English and Spanish, tours leave every 30 minutes from 1000-1830 except 1400 and 1430*. The tour takes you through some furnished rooms, with some excellent 17th-century coffered ceilings and a large collection of paintings. There's a good Luca Giordano, several mediocre portraits of family members, a Goya of the Ronda bullring, and an Assumption by Murillo, not one of his better works. The Apotheosis of Hercules is well painted on the ceiling in one room; it was designed and partly painted by Pacheco, whose daughter married Velásquez.

● *In the square outside the house is a statue of Zurbarán, brushes and palette in hand. Just behind the house stands a church called San Esteban. If you're lucky, it'll be open (from about 1800 is best) and you can admire two of the artist's works, of Saint Peter and Saint Paul, in the* retablo, *among other good paintings from his school.*

★ **Crooked mediaeval streets**

Best

- •C Lope de Rueda
- •C Judería
- •C Leviés
- •C Siete Revueltas
- •C de los Navarros

Iglesia de San Pedro

Plaza San Pedro s/n. *Mon-Sat 0900-1130, 1900-2030,
Sun 0930-1230, 1900-2030. Free.* Map 4, L5, p255

Started in the 14th century, San Pedro has been extensively
modified over the centuries. The brick Mudéjar tower clashes
with the severe stone portal, but inside is an excellent *retablo*
with scenes from the first pope's life. Locals say that if you manage
to spot the hidden bird in the tiled panel to the right of the front
door, it'll bring good luck. In reality, if you don't spot it, it'll mean
a pricey visit to the optometrist. To the left of the door, in a little
plaza is a statue to Santa Angela de la Cruz, a local nun who, along
with the sisterhood she founded (often seen on the streets with
their distinctive chocolate robes), did much good work with the
poor in the 20th century. To Seville's delight, she was canonized
in Madrid in May 2003; the council reacted with unprecedented
haste, and the name of the square and street were changed from
'Sor' to 'Santa' in the blink of an eye.

● *A few metres up Calle Doña María Coronel, duck into the
Convento de Santa Inés for some tasty* dulces *sold by the nuns
through the traditional revolving cylinder. A few paces further along
this street, there's a modern exhibition centre tucked beside the
convent; there's often good contemporary art on display here.*

Museo Palacio de Lebrija

C Cuna 8, **T** 954 218 183, www.palaciodelebrija.com
Mon-Fri 1030-1300, 1630-1900 (1700-1930 in summer),
Sat 1000-1300, €3.60/€6.60 ground/both floors. Map 2, A2, p250

The Countess of Lebrija (1851-1938) was an interesting lady who
travelled widely in Asia, North Africa, and Europe during her long
life. She and her husband both had a great interest in art and
archaeology and she strove to purchase and excavate as much
material from the site of Itálica as possible. This material, along
with numerous other *objets d'art* and other trappings of wealth, are
on display in this pretty palace, which she completely remodelled in
the early 20th century as a repository for her collections.

The upper floor is accessed by a good guided tour, *Spanish,*
English, French which leaves every 30 mins; apart from the elegance
of the salons and their diverse decoration, items of interest include
an early 16th-century tryptych, several intricate cabinets, French
porcelain and three gorgeous trunks that the Condesa used to lug
around the world with her. The ground floor lacks a little by
comparison; the archaeological material is displayed in cases, but
there is little information and no context. Overall, the quantity is
more impressive than the quality, although a restorer's touch would
highlight the better examples. Most impressive are some of the
mosaics from Itálica and the bright *azulejos* in the back chamber.

Iglesia del Salvador

Plaza del Salvador s/n, **T** 954 211 679. *Closed until late 2003.*
Normally Mon-Sat 1830-2100, Sun 1030-1400, 1900-2100. Free.
Map 2, B3, p250

The enormous red brick façade of this baroque church dominates
the pretty, but rundown, square it's on, now a lively venue for
evening bars and *botellón*. Started in the 17th century, it suffered
numerous changes of plan over the years, but is still an impressive

sight. It's hard to get a good glimpse of the typically colourful cupola, but the spacious interior has some fine artworks to compensate, including the respected Cristo de la Pasión, by the father of Semana Santa sculpture, Juan Martínez Montañés and a highly ornate Churrigueresque *retablo*. The *patio de naranjos* is an unexpected find in a church, but the building used to be a mosque, and the courtyard is a remnant from those days. While you're here, check out Plaza de Jesús de la Pasión behind the church, with an attractive row of jewellers' and bridal shops, one of which is in an ornately tiled and turreted building at its end.

Iglesia de la Magdalena

C San Pablo 10, **T** 954 229 603. *Mon-Sat 0730-1100, 1830-2130, Sun 0730-1300. Free. Bus 3. Map 3, C8, p252*

This important baroque parish church is one of the city's biggest and hard to miss if you're strolling around in the vicinity. Its roof and cupola are highly decorated with bright ceramics while its western façade is adorned with big blue sundials, although they're a little difficult to see as the street is narrow. Have a look around between Masses and you'll appreciate the spacious baroque interior covered with wall paintings, many executed by Lucas Valdés. The high main *retablo* is typical of the Churrigueresque style and is centred on Mary Magdalene holding a crucifix. There are many smaller altarpieces around, all heavily gilded and containing icons much venerated by locals. The highlights are two Zurbaráns; they are in the side chapel of Virgen de las Flores. Both are scenes of St Dominic; the stranger of the two depicts the moment when the Virgin appeared to a monastic community in Italy with a painting of the saint to serve as a model for all future representations of him.

★ Museo de Bellas Artes de Sevilla

Plaza del Museo 9, **T** 954 221 829,
www.juntadeandalucia.es/cultura *Tue 1500-2000,
Wed-Sat 0900-2000, Sun 0900-1400. Free for EU citizens
(€1.50 for others). Bus C3, C4. Map 3, A7, p252*

Seville's major art gallery is a must-see, picturesquely housed in a
17th-18th century convent. This is appropriate enough, as most of
the collection comes from monasteries stripped of their possess-
ions in the Disentailment Act of 1835. The Sevillan School of
painting was the dominant artistic force in Spain's "Golden Age"
and is represented here, offset by peaceful and pretty tiled patios.

Thoughtfully laid out and thankfully uncluttered, the collection
begins with the 15th century, where a pair of wooden Christs by
Pedro Millán and an Ascension by Bernardo Martorell stand out.
The next room includes a huge Renaissance tryptych of Calvary by
Frans Francken and an excellent *retablo* piece from the monastery
of San Agustín by Martín de Vos showing the awakening dead
being sorted by angels and demons. There's also an El Greco; a
good portrait of his own son.

In the early years of the 17th century, two distinct styles were
evident in Sevillian painting; naturalism and mannerism, but these
were gradually brought together as the century progressed. The
latter style is well represented here by a selection of Francisco
Pacheco's works. A portrait by the master Diego Velásquez
(Pacheco's son-in-law) of a gentleman against a brooding sky
is also in this section. Room IV has works of another Mannerist,
Alonso Vásquez, including, appropriately, a series on San Pedro
Nolasco, who founded the original monastery on this site.

The former convent church is an awesome space with an
elaborate painted ceiling. Here we see the evolution of the Seville
School to its peak; the works of Zurbarán and Murillo. Although
the former is represented in this chamber by a suitably imposing
heavenly Father and his large, famous Apotheosis of St Thomas

"Mi infancia son recuerdos de un patio de Sevilla/
y un huerto claro donde madura el limonero"

"My infancy is memories of a patio in Seville
And a bright garden where the lemon tree grows"

Antonio Machado, Retrato *text.*

Aquinas, there are more of his works upstairs; this room belongs to Murillo, whose statue graces the square outside the museum. Most of his works on display here come from the former Capuchin monastery. The city's patrons, Santa Justa and Santa Rufina, hold the Giralda in one famous work, while a tender San Felix and child, St Francis' dream of the crucified Christ, and the famous "Virgin of the Napkin" who holds a wide-eyed Christ child, are other noteworthy pieces. While mannerist traces remain in his early work, Murillo evolves into a complete baroque style characterized by intense religious fervour, usually centred around a central gaze or glance of striking power or emotion. There are more Murillos upstairs, and a long gallery devoted to Juan de Valdés Leal (1622-1690), who has a series of monks in a lovely, at times, caricatural style.

Zurbarán, a little out of context, is represented in Room X. In the corridor outside is perhaps his most powerful work here, a Crucifixion of incredible solitude and force, with Christ, head down, seemingly chiselled from rock. Also here, look out for the shadow of a lion expertly painted at the feet of San Jerónimo. Zurbarán's works provide a good opportunity to study some real faces from the period; he often used monks as models, particularly in the Cartuja de las Cuevas series in an adjoining room. His love of white cloth, expertly executed, is also a feature. Many of his works, though few of those here, are poor in quality, rush jobs churned out on contract, but his masterpieces elevate him as high as any figure in western art. After these heights, Seville's painting declined along with the city, but a curious series from the old tobacco factory by Domingo Martínez depicts ornate processional floats. There's also a late portrait by Goya.

The 19th- and 20th-century rooms have works by Sevillan proto-Impressionist Gonzalo Bilbao as well as a scene from Don Quijote by José Moreno Carbonero. The haunted Romantic poet Gustavo Adolfo Bécquer is sensitively portrayed by his brother Valeriano, while two good portraits by the Basque painter Ignacio Zuloaga and a fiesta scene by Gustavo Bacarisos round off the fine collection.

● *By the museum is a chapel of a* cofradía, *the Hermandad del Museo. The emotive Christ was so admired that the sculptor Antonio Ruíz was allegedly ordered to give up the moulds so more could be produced. He refused and threw himself into the Guadalquivir with the moulds. Cross Calle Alfonso XII and head into the web of streets around Calle Alfaqueque, some of La Macarena's nicest, with cobbles and noble old buildings. Plaza Doña Teresa Enriquez has a 16th-century stone crucifix in a little plaza next to a bright baroque church.*

★ Calle Sierpes and the Shopping Zone
Bus 21, 23, 25, 26, 40.   Map 2, A2, p250

Seville's major streets for classy shopping are Sierpes, Tetuán, Velásquez, Cuna and O'Donnell. It's a fascinating stroll around this area and there's an encouragingly low number of chain stores, giving the zone a particularly local character. Shops selling fans, shawls and other Seville fashion essentials abound. The prime fashion labels can be bought here, including Victorio & Lucchino, the brand of a successful Sevillian designer and his Córdoban partner who have had much success in the world of catwalks and supermodels. On Calle Tetuán is a charming old advertisement for Studebaker cars in colourful Triana tiles.

Iglesia de San José
*C Jovellanos s/n.   Mon-Sat 1830-2100, Sun 0800-1300.
Bus 40.   Map 2, B2, p250*

This small, parish church is just off Calle Sierpes and is busy in the evenings with parishioners rustling in with their shopping bags after the *compras*. While the San Antonio in the side aisle is held in high esteem and much prayed-to and petitioned, of most interest is the main *retablo*, an extraordinary sight with its two side panels and bristling with cherubs; it could be a production of *A Midsummer Night's Dream* in gold. Atop, God overlooks Joseph

holding his Son's hand, while below is a Madonna and Child.
It's one of the more surprising and breathtaking sights in
Seville, housed as it is behind an unremarkable, if cheery façade.

★ Ayuntamiento (Town Hall)

Plaza Nueva s/n, **T** 954 590 101. *Tue-Thu tours at 1730 and 1800,
Sat 1000-1300. Free. Bus 40, 21, 23, 25, 26. Map 2, C2, p250*

Formerly the site of one of Seville's most important monasteries
founded by the Franciscans shortly after the *Reconquista*. Carlos V
built a small town hall up against its walls in the 16th century;
when Spanish monasteries were disentailed in 1835, it was
decided to demolish the Convento de San Francisco, expand the
tiny *ayuntamiento*, and create a new civic space: the Plaza Nueva.
As such, the building has two distinct sections, a Plateresque and a
neoclassical (as well as some more recent annexes). From Plaza San
Francisco, you can admire the superbly intricate stonework of the
original 16th-century building. The architect of the newer structure
thought he'd better continue with the Plateresque design to
ensure harmony, but was stopped in his tracks by outraged
neoclassicists appalled at the perceived flippancy; the Plateresque
stonework thus comes to an abrupt and jagged end.

The interior, entered through the sober façade on Plaza Nueva,
is a revelation, *bring passport or ID to enter*. An excellent
volunteer-guided tour, *currently Spanish only, but it's worth doing
even if you don't understand the commentary*, will take you around
the chambers of the original edifice, which has some breathtaking
Renaissance stonework that still features some Gothic influences.
The lower council chamber is entered through a dignified doorway
crowned with a depiction of Fernando III; inside there's an amazing
coffered stone ceiling with busts of 36 monarchs in the coffers,
finishing with Carlos V himself in one corner, complete with
imperial crown. You ascend to the top floor via an elegant staircase
with a Renaissance cupola and works by Zurbarán and Lucas

Valdés. Notable works of art in the upper council chamber include a Zurbarán Inmaculada and a sketch by Murillo as well as numerous 19th-century works. A small museum contains replicas of the Tartessian hoard, displays of Roman coins, and gifts to the city from all corners of the world; this room was once a gallery from which to watch the bullfights, processions, and *autos de fé* (the Inquisition's trials) that took place in the Plaza de San Francisco.

La Macarena

*Once one of the poorest slums in the peninsula, these days La Macarena's an enticing web of narrow streets and numerous churches. One of these is home to Seville's best-loved Virgin, **La Esperanza de la Macarena** (see box p84). She gives her name to many of Seville's women, one of whom was the subject of the best-selling Latin hit of all time, by the ageing duo Los del Río. Still a working-class zone, La Macarena is home to much of Seville's alternative culture, its best markets and much of its most interesting nightlife. Well away from the touristed areas, it also makes a great place to wander around by day with numerous intriguing corners, solid neighbourhood tapas bars, and original shops.*

▸▸ *See Sleeping p122, Eating and drinking p141, Bars and clubs p154*

 Sights

★ Convento de Santa Paula
C Santa Paula s/n, **T** 954 536 330. *Tue-Sun 1000-1300.*
€2. Bus 10, C3, C4. *Map 4, I8, p255*

There's an air of mystery about visiting this cloistered convent; knock at the door and be admitted after an age and then get shown around by a knowledgeable old nun with a twinkle in her eye. It's the home of 42 nuns; the building dates from the 15th century and was once the house of the founder of the order before being expanded into a convent in the 16th century. It contains many pieces of art of varying quality and some fine, faded, but wholly original, 15th-century *artesonado* ceilings. There's a gorgeous patio and a tiled doorway, a work of Niculoso Pisano. On either side of the church are a pair of sculptures by Martínez Montañés of John the Baptist and John the apostle, while some Alonso Cano works are also present.

Iglesia de San Marcos
Plaza de San Marcos. *Bus 10, C3, C4. Map 4, I7, p255*

This Gothic-Mudéjar church, once a mosque, has an excellent façade, with a toothed Gothic portal, delicate Mudéjar blind arcading above, and the bearded evangelist himself atop. However, it is most notable for its slim tower, which is very similar in style to the Giralda. It's adorned with very attractive brickwork and a series of windows that increase in size as the tower rises. The interior features some horseshoe arches, preserved despite extensive Civil War damage. Behind the church is the pretty Plaza Santa Isabel, with a fountain and trees; the convent church here has a cloister and a main *retablo* by the famous sculptor Juan de Mesa.

Iglesia de San Luís de los Franceses
C San Luís s/n, **T** 954 214 024. *Tue-Sat 0900-1400, Fri-Sat also 1700-2000. Free. Bus 10. Map 4, G7, p255*

If you're just meandering down this interesting street, the flamboyant façade of this former Jesuit college will snap you out of your reverie. Although the road is too narrow to really appreciate the architecture, the front is a baroque masterpiece with scores of Churrigueresque features. Between the twin belltowers, carved with the four Evangelists, pairs of cherubs perch among the foliated and corkscrewed pilasters. Although it's difficult to get a good view of the dome from the outside, it's colourfully decked out in red and yellow, a contrast with the ceramic tiles atop the belltowers. Inside the circular interior are several *retablos*, the finest is the main one, inlaid with blue ceramic and centred around a small Madonna painting; look out also for the massive Zurbarán painting depicting the saint, who was king of France in his earthly days. The ceiling frescoes in the dome are also impressive; an ornate mirror is on hand to help you appreciate them.

Iglesia de Santa Marina
C San Luís s/n. *Bus 10. Map 4, F7, p254*

This 14th-century church is similar in style to San Marcos further down the road; this too has a Mudéjar tower, albeit more squat and more militaristic. The portal is the most impressive feature, with a Gothic arched doorway surrounded with Mudéjar foliation, sculptures of Christ and the Madonna that some think pre-date the church, and 14 weathered roaring lions.

Plaza del Pumarejo
Bus C1, C2, C3, C4. Map 4, E6, p254

A shady spot frequented by some real barrio characters. One side of the square is taken up by the **Casa Pumarejo**, a lovely old palace currently in disrepair. The patio is decked out with some stunning *azulejos*; locals have been mounting a campaign to rescue and restore the building, but to their displeasure, it now seems likely that it will be converted into a hotel. Some good simple bars are on the square; good places to meet locals.

● *Seville has a long and proud anarchist tradition dating back to the 19th century. The legacy lives on around the corner from Plaza del Pumarejo at Calle Antonia Saénz 12, a famous squat called **Casas Viejas**. There are frequent punk and rock concerts, as well as regular free workshops. Upcoming events are posted on the front door.*

★ Las Murallas
Bus C1, C2, C3, C4. Map 4, D6, p254

Seville's walls were probably originally, at least, partially Roman, perhaps built by Julius Caesar when he governed the region. The Moors made them formidable again; with the circumference of some six kms defended by 166 towers, a moat, and jagged castellation.

Basílica de la Macarena
C Bécquer 1, **T** 954 370 195. *Mon-Sun 0930-1300, 1700-2000 (Semana Santa 0900-1500 most days). Free (€2.80 for museum).*
Bus C1, C2, C3, C4. Map 4, D6, p254

The home of Seville's most-adored Mother of God is a fairly recent construction; the first stone was laid by Pope Pius XII in the 1940s. Its cheery yellow colour matches the gateway next to it, a reconstruction of what was once one of the main entrances into the city. Inside, the Virgin (see box, p84) takes pride of place in the *retablo*; the Christ from the other *paso* stands in front of her. The interior of the church is decorated with murals depicting scenes from the Virgin's life and popes who have been significant to the basilica's young existence. There's also a museum and popular gift shop.

● *If you're hungry and you like the words "authentic", "budget", "no-frills" and "tasty", follow Calle San Luis from the Basilica towards Plaza del Pumarejo. At number 99 you'll find Bar Ría de Vigo, which puts on a decent sized plate of their* plato del día *for €2.10.*

Hospital de las Cinco Llagas
C Parlamento de Andalucía s/n, **T** 954 592 100.
Bus C1, C2, C3, C4. Map 4, B6, p254

This massive rectangular building was built in the 16th century and is said to have been the biggest hospital in the world at the time. The sober façade is long and impressive but these days the

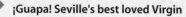

▶ ¡Guapa! Seville's best loved Virgin

La Virgen de la Esperanza de la Macarena, to give her her full name, lives in a small basilica by the Puerta de Macarena.

Although the Esperanza de Triana pushes her close, La Macarena has won the war for Seville's hearts. Her picture adorns thousands of bars, taxis, and wallets, and her *paso* is the most eagerly awaited of Semana Santa.

After the Christ figure has passed, with its garrison of Roman soldiers with feathered plumes, the crowd eagerly awaits the first glimpse. A lull falls over all ages and a palpable respect is in the air. Necks crane to see the Macarena's new outfit, and shouts of "¡guapa!" (referring to physical beauty) fill the air. The tears on La Macarena's face reflect her gleaming crown and halo. On her breast are five emeralds that were a gift to her from the bullfighter Joselito, who adored her. When he was killed in 1920, La Macarena dressed in black the following Easter to mourn him.

patients have been replaced by politicians; it's the seat of Andalucía's regional parliament. The *diputados* sit in the former church of the building, which also boasts four large patios.

Cementerio de San Fernando

Av Medina y Galnares s/n. *Daily 0800-1730. Free. Bus 10 from Plaza Encarnación (get off straight after a big roundabout five minutes after passing the Hospital de las Cinco Llagas). Map 1, A7, p248*

Further past the hospital is Seville's massive main cemetery, fronted by an elegant series of neo-Mudéjar buildings and with a gateway built for entrance and exit by carriages. You could wander for days in the vast expanse – there's even a small Muslim cemetery at the back – but some tombs of interest are near the gate on the left. There's an area of bullfighters and flamenco artists; you can't miss the elaborate tomb of Joselito, dead at only 25, but perhaps the greatest *torero* of all time (see box p59). His memorial is an elaborate sculptural assembly of a coffin borne by mourners, one of whom carries an icon of his beloved Virgen de la Macarena. His brother Rafael is also buried here, as is the famous Sánchez Mejías. Opposite is the tomb of a more recent great, Francisco Rivera, while the actress and singer Juanita Reina stands tall nearby, on the other side of a grave of Falangist dead from the Civil War. In the next aisle on the left is another bullfighter, Juan Belmonte; in less tolerant times he wouldn't have made it to consecrated ground, for he died by his own hand.

★ Alameda de Hércules
Bus 13, 14. Map 4, G3, p255

This long avenue lined with planes and poplars is the centre of Seville's alternative, punk, and anarchist scene. Once a marsh, it was drained in the 16th century and adorned at both ends with Roman columns; upon the taller of the two were placed sculptures of Hercules, who is said to have founded Seville, and Julius Caesar, whose presence as governor of the province is considerably more certain. Once a red-light district (there's still a little going on), it is now lined with cafés and bars. On one side is the **Casa de las Sirenas**, a lovely early 20th-century mansion. On Sunday mornings (and a little on Thursday), there's a lively flea market here; while Seville's busiest and oldest market, "El Jueves", takes place on Thursday morning a couple of blocks away on Calle Feria.

! For much of the 16th century, Seville was Europe's
• fourth-largest city after Paris, Naples and Venice.

Calle Santa Clara and Plaza San Lorenzo
Map 4, H1, p255

This area tucked between the Alameda de Hércules and the river has three interesting buildings to visit. At the northernmost end of Calle Santa Clara is the **Convento de San Clemente**, whose church and pleasant cloister now hold changing exhibitions. There are still nuns here; you can buy their *dulces* around the side on Calle Reposo. At no 40 is the **Convento de Santa Clara**. The *dulces* from here are sold at no 50. On Plaza San Lorenzo is the **Iglesia de San Lorenzo y Jesús del Gran Poder**, most notable for the 17th-century sculpture of Christ by Juan de Mesa in a side chapel. It's a breathtaking piece; Jesus looks utterly careworn and harrowed.

Isla de la Cartuja

The clay-rich Isla de la Cartuja was a centre for potters' workshops in bygone centuries but was more or less derelict until the city decided to make it the site of the World Expo in 1992. Predictably for such an event, costs went through the roof and the city was left with massive debts and a huge space filled with modern buildings. While the university use some of them, there's a popular theme park (see p197) and a few bars and auditoriums, much of the site is decaying amid administrative wrangling and failed development proposals. Still, it's interesting to wander around; pick a weekday, as most of the site is depressingly empty at weekends. At the southern end is the massive ocean-liner profile of the headquarters of the Andalucían Junta. The monastery where Columbus once came for contemplation is now a good contemporary arts centre and there's an excellent park at the northern end of the island.

▸▸ *See Eating and drinking p142, Bars and clubs p157*

Sights

Monasterio de la Cartuja/
Centro Andaluz de Arte Contemporáneo

Av Américo Vespucio 2, **T** 955 037 070, www.juntadeandalucia.es/ cultura *Oct-Mar, Tue-Fri 1000-2000, Sat 1100-2100, Sun 1000-1500; Apr-Jun and Sep, Tue-Fri 1000-2100, Sat 1100-2000, Sun 1100-1500; Jul-Aug, Mon-Fri 1000-2300, Sat 1100-1500. €3.01; audio-guide available. Bus 1/C2. Map 1, E1, p248*

Ceramics have been made here since ancient times; it was in a pottery in the 13th century that the Virgin appeared and a shrine was built. It was later developed into this important monastery, a favourite of Seville's wealthy and powerful in the Golden Age. Columbus came here to pray and contemplate his next voyages; when he died his remains lay here for 23 years. In the Peninsular War, the arch-desecrator of Spanish cultural heritage, Maréchal Soult, stationed troops here, who badly damaged the buildings; once the monks were expelled some 20 years later, it was in a poor state and was picked up cheaply by Charles Pickman, a British businessman, who set up a ceramics factory and lived there. Pickman generally respected the monastic buildings, though all were put to use, and the huge brick kilns and chimneys still dominate the site.

Renovated by the Seville authorities, it became the Royal Pavilion of Expo 92 and is now partly given over to a good contemporary art museum. First, visit the church itself with a small cloister, a refectory with a beautiful coffered ceiling and the well-carved tombs of the powerful Ribera family. The permanent collection (not all of which is always on display) has some excellent pieces, mostly by Andalucían artists. Look out for Guillermo Pérez Villalta's series on the four elements, which speaks powerfully about the fate of the Moors and their cultural contribution to Andalucía.

Pabellón de la Energía Viva

C Marie Curie s/n, **T** 954 467 146,
www.pabellondelaenergiaviva.com *Mon-Sat 1000-1900,
Sun 1100-1900. €5.60. Bus C1, C2. Map 1, B2, p248*

One of the prettiest of the Expo pavilions, the Hungarian structure
has recently been transformed into this interactive environmental
museum. Shaped like an upturned boat, the towers represent the
world's eight principal religions.

Parque del Alamillo

*Daily 0800-2200, 0800-2400 summer. Bus E5 from
Puente de la Barqueta. Map 1, A3, p248*

Seville's biggest park is a good spot to head to for a picnic, a bit
of exercise, or some relaxed summer strolling or sunbathing. It's
a popular destination with *sevillanos* at weekends. There's a lake,
and in summer there are terraced *chiringuitos* to have a drink, and
a cycle hire place. Beyond here is the Estadio Olímpico, built in the
vain hope of hosting the 2008 Olympics.

★ The Calatrava bridges

Map 1, C3, p248 and Map 1, A5, p248

Two of the bridges that link La Cartuja with central Seville are
works of the inspirational Valencian architect Santiago Calatrava.
Designed for the Expo, they quickly became popular icons of the
city. The closest to town is the Puente de la Barqueta, an elegant
arch offset by perpendicular cables. From here you get a superb
view of the next one, the sublime Puente del Alamillo. Drawing
themes from birds in flight as well as Viking longships, the bridge
features a single angled upright at one end, linked to the other end
by streaming cables; it's an impressive sight indeed.

New Town Boulevards

The wealthy homes in the eastern suburbs around Nervión are in contrast to some of the poorer barrios in other directions; this area is home to some striking modern architecture and much of the town's commerce. There are some good nightlife options around here (see box, p158) and, as a result of all the offices, some excellent lunch-hour tapas. There's good shopping around Calle de Luís Montoto, where there's also the remains of an old Moorish aqueduct that used to bring water to the city from Carmona, 36 kilometres distant. Seville's two football teams, between whom absolutely no love is lost, are based out in these parts, Sevilla FC to the east of town, and Real Betis considerably further away to the south.

▸▸ *See Eating and drinking p143, Bars and clubs p157*

 Sights

★ La Estación de Santa Justa
Av Kansas City s/n. *Bus 32. Map 1, F8, p248*

Named after one of the city's two patron saints, this modern train station was completed in 1991. Designed by the local architectural duo of Antonio Cruz and Antonio Ortiz, it's typical of their unadorned modernism while still recalling the Muslim era with its imposing brick façade.

Cruz del Campo
Av Luís Montoto s/n. *Bus 21, 24, 27. Map 1, H7, p249*

The "cross of the fields" is a Gothic/Mudéjar stone crucifix on Avenida Luís Montoto, sheltered by a brick pavilion. When the Marquis of Tarifa returned from the Holy Land and designed his Casa de Pilatos, he decided to establish a re-enactment in Seville of

Phenomenal architecture
The Santa Justa train station with its high speed trains linking Andalucía to the capital.

▶ A serious rivalry

At least until you wedge them into the stadium on derby day, Seville folk mostly have a very relaxed football rivalry; groups of friends will often be half *bético* and half *sevillista*. This doesn't apply to the clubs themselves though; they hate each other. Sevilla FC formed in 1905, but when the board refused to sanction the signing of a working-class player in 1909, two of the members resigned in protest and formed Betis. Since that moment, Real Betis have been solidly associated with the left of the political divide and Sevilla with the right.

In the aftermath of the Civil War, the Soviet Union was outraged when Sevilla poached the Betis manager, but in more recent times the relationship has deteriorated even further. In 1978 Sevilla allegedly threw a game against lowly Hércules in order to ensure the relegation of Betis. Betis were less successful in 1999 when their chairman was accused of paying Albacete players to get a result at Sevilla, thus damaging their chances of promotion to the top division, where Betis were enjoying sneering at them from. Albacete got the result, but Sevilla went up anyway. They had some bitter revenge in 2000. Already relegated, Sevilla appeared to lose deliberately at home to Oviedo, who thus saved themselves and relegated Betis.

Living up to their catchcry "Viva er Beti manque pierda" (long live Betis, even if they lose) an undaunted Betis (and Sevilla) are back in Primera action.

Christ's journey to Calvary. Starting at his house, he marked out a route, which ended here, thus replicating the distance Christ supposedly walked. The Cruz del Campo is rather forgotten about now, but in a way, however, it's Seville's best known landmark, as the ubiquitous Cruzcampo beer is brewed in an attractive factory a stone's throw from the cross it's named after.

Estadio Sánchez Pizjuan

Av Eduardo Dato s/n. **T** 954 535 353, www.sevillafc.es

Bus 5, 22, 23, 32. Map 1, I8, p249

The home of Sevilla FC is adorned with a massive tiled wall with the pennants of the famous club sides that have played here. Despite the intense and often downright nasty rivalry, even Real Betis get a mention! See p187 for more details of matches and box on p92 for more on the city's two clubs.

San Bernardo

C Santo Rey s/n. *Bus 23. Map 1, I7, p249*

This church gives its name to a small barrio around it. The church itself is big, bright and yellow with an attractive tiled dome and belltower. The church is home to a Semana Santa cofradía; behind the church is a large old armaments factory.

● *Just east of the church begins the pretty neo-Moorish park, the Jardines de Buhaira. It's a nice place, and there's an especially good tapas bar here, La Huerta (see p144). Stop off for a snack in the shade of its fantastic terrace.*

Listings

Museums and galleries

- **Archivo de las Indias** This contains fascinating displays on the discovery and administration of the Americas, p42.
- **Casa de la Memoria de Al-Andalus** Flamenco venue and small museum dedicated to the glory days of the Muslim city, p49.
- **Casa de Pilatos** Sumptuous Renaissance mansion dotted with classical statuary, p70.
- **Casa-Museo de Murillo** There's not a great deal to see at but it's worth popping in just to see where Murillo hung out, p49.
- **Hospital de la Caridad** The chapel contains as many fine pictures as it's possible to see in a space this size, p60.
- **Hospital de los Venerables** The chapel has a fine collection of art and there are usually excellent temporary exhibitions, p46.
- **La Maestranza** Seville's bullring and museum with some interesting exhibits for enthusiasts of the activity, p58.
- **Monasterio de la Cartuja/Centro Andaluz de Arte Contemporáneo** A building with an interesting history and a small but attractive collection of contemporary art, p87.
- **Museo Arqueológico** Superb finds from the Roman site of Itálica are the highlight here, p55.
- **Museo de Artes y Costumbres Populares de Sevilla** Excellent ethnographic museum, a cut above most of its kind, p55.
- **Museo de Bellas Artes** Seville's art gallery has a superb collection from the golden age of painting, p75.
- **Museo de Carruajes** A change from the art, this has a selection of horse carriages on display, p69.
- **Museo Palacio de Lebrija** A *palacio* with a higgledy-piggledy collection of archaeological finds, paintings and furniture, p73.
- **Pabellón de la Energía Viva** A newly opened environmental museum in the former Hungarian Expo pavilion, p88.
- **Torre del Oro** A mediocre maritime museum fills this pretty Moorish tower, p57.

Itálica 97

The ruins of what was once one of the Roman Empire's largest cities. Excellent mosaics and an amphitheatre are the highlights.

Alcalá de Guadaira 100

A seriously impressive crumbly Moorish castle is the main reason to visit this town on the city outskirts.

Carmona 100

This hilltop town is entered via an imposing bastion 2,500 years old in parts. On the edge of town is an important Roman necropolis.

Ecija 102

Once the home of wealthy landowners, who adorned their town with beautiful baroque church towers and elegant palaces.

Jerez de la Frontera 102

Aristocratic Jerez is the home of sherry and the finest of Spanish horses.

Córdoba 106

A Moorish city – its sublime Mezquita preserves some of the atmosphere from those heady days.

Itálica

*While Seville likes to talk up its Roman heritage, it's important to remember that for a long time it was but a satellite town to mighty Itálica an hour's march (at ultra-brisk legionary pace) away on the other side of the Guadalquivir. While most of the haphazardly-excavated riches are to be found in Seville itself, the site is worth the short bus trip if only for a peaceful (if sunbaked) wander among the meadows and broken stone. The large **amphitheatre** is the most impressive structure on view and the wealthy season-ticket holders lived nearby, in palatial houses still decorated with fine mosaics. If you can, visit the excellent archaeological museum in Seville before coming here, as otherwise it can be difficult to appreciate just how significant a site it is.*

Sights

★ The ruins

Santiponce village, **T** 955 997 376. *Tue-Sat 0830-2030, Sun 0900-1500. Free for EU citizens, €1.50. Casal bus from Plaza de Armas bus station (platform 34) to Santiponce, € 0.94 each way (9 km, 25 mins), every 20-30 mins weekdays and Sat mornings, every hour Sat afternoons and Sun. By car follow the N630 north to Mérida across the Puente Cristo de la Expiración. Map Around Seville*

It's hard to believe, wandering around the ruins of Itálica, that this was once one of the Roman Empire's largest and most important cities. In truth, little of it has been excavated; what you can walk around today is the partially revealed remains of the *nova urbs* (new town; a relative term these days) built by Hadrian in the early second century AD, while the *vetus urbs* (old town) lies under the village of Santiponce. It was originally built by Publius Cornelius Scipio in 206 BC; one of the Italian (not Roman) regiments of his army had a rough time of it during the battle against the Carthaginians at Illipa and he decided to build a settlement for them to let them heal up and ease the threat of mutiny. It grew rapidly and in time became the most important Roman city in the region, birthplace of the emperor Trajan and perhaps his protegé Hadrian, who certainly grew up here.

Digs of one sort or another have been going on here for centuries; there's plenty of Roman stone at the sprawling 14th-century monastery of San Isidoro down the road (worth a visit), and several aristocrats have stuck their spades in, including the Duke of Wellington during the Napoleonic wars. Many Sevillian mansions are adorned with finds from the site, but for the highest concentration, don't come here, but visit the superb archaeological museum in Seville (see p55).

While it's a pleasant place to wander around, with birds, bees, and acres of flowering weeds, there's not a huge amount to see here (and the information given is paltry), but what's here is very good, particularly the huge amphitheatre near the entrance, which seated 20,000. Although much of the seating has been removed over the years, the terraces are still very clear, as are the stairways, and the large sunken area in the middle (thought to have had a central daïs erected over it for use in gladiatorial combats). A fascinating find here is displayed in a side chamber: a bronze tablet inscribed with various norms for gladiatorial combat imposed by Marcus Aurelius and his son (who else but Commodus, Russell Crowe's sworn enemy in *Gladiator*).

The other highlights of a visit are the mosaics on display on the floors of some of the excavated houses. The House of Neptune has one of these; the centre features sea creatures, including the god himself, while the outer edges depict a Nilotic hunting scene; it's not without its humour, as the large crane doing an injury to a hunter's backside attests. There's a statue of the god-emperor Trajan near here; it's thought that the whole of this section of the city was built by Hadrian in his predecessor's honour. The House of the Birds also has some excellent mosaics, two of which colourfully feature an array of the feathered tribe. The House of the Planetarium has perhaps the finest piece, with portraits of the seven divinities who gave their name to the Roman week.

It's hotter here than Seville, and there's not much shade, but thankfully there are several good bars and restaurants clustered around the entrance. If you're not exhausted yet, turn right out of the entrance and up the hill a couple of minutes to check out the partially restored Roman theatre (there's a tourist information point here). Don't bother with the small bathhouse nearby, but if you have time, investigate the monastery further up the road, cosecrated in 1298. The return bus passes the entrance to this, so you won't have to retrace your steps.

East of Seville

*The scorching plains of Seville province are still divided into huge estates, latifundias, which produce, among other things, two Spanish icons: olives and fighting bulls. Around this parched and mesmeric landscape are dotted towns which give a much different view of Andalucía to Seville. Many were important fortresses during the gruelling wars of the Reconquista; later they were embellished by the local aristocracy who had grown wealthy from their lands, farmed by peasants for minimal reward. The result is an engaging mixture of the grand and the humble, with grandiose façades and muscly fortresses towering over earthy bars where the sophistication of Seville can seem very far away. Another attraction is the fascinating **Roman necropolis** at Carmona, a well-excavated site outside the heavily-defended hilltop town.*

▸▸ *See Sleeping p123, Eating and drinking p145, Festivals p169, Kids p198*

◉ Sights

Alcalá de Guadaira

Buses roughly every 20 mins from Av Portugal by Bar Citroën (after 2100 they run from the Prado San Sebastián bus station); €0.95. Map Around Seville

Now basically a suburb of Seville, the friendly village of Alcalá is worth visiting for its muscular Moorish fortress, a construction of the Almohads. It's on a huge scale and is seriously impressive, if getting a bit crumbly. It's fun to poke around, but it's basically a shell; little remains inside the walls.

Carmona

Casal runs buses hourly on the hour weekdays from the Prado de San Sebastián station in Seville (platform 25, at far end on the left) from 0700-2200; Sat, 10 buses daily; Sun, 7 buses daily; 50 mins, €2. Map Around Seville

The town of Carmona, 36 kilometres east of Seville, has been an important settlement since the Chalcolithic period, largely due to its commanding hilltop position. It's an easy day or half-day trip from the city, with which it has good bus connections.

There's only one feasible way up to the hilltop and this has been fortified since the Bronze Age. Successive conquering powers; the Phoenicians, the Romans, the Moors, and the Castillians have left a legacy in the impressive **Alcázar** fortress guarding the way in. Looming over the narrow entrance gate known as the Puerta de Sevilla, the complex is bulky and impressive, and preserves structures from all these periods.

The tourist office is located here, *Mon-Sat 1000-1800, Sun 1000-1500*; who will furnish you with a map of the town. It's worth visiting the complex itself, *same opening hours; €2/€1 students*, to admire the heavy fortifications and gain a view from the tower over the rooftops and the fertile plains below.

At the top of the old town is another Alcázar, part of which has been converted into a *parador*. Also, within the walled area are several churches: **Santa María la Mayor** preserves the former mosque's **Patio de Naranjos** and has a good 16th-century *retablo*, while **San Pedro** has an attractive Mudéjar tower. There are good tapas options around the shady main square **Plaza de San Fernando**; it's also worth seeking out the **Plaza de Abastos**, a satisfying hidden space used for morning markets. There are also good accommodation options in the old town (see Sleeping).

Walking down the hill from the main gate, you'll come to a long square, **Paseo del Estatuto**, (where the bus stops). At the far end of this, take the middle of the three streets, which after 10 minutes will bring you to the **Roman Necropolis**, *Tue-Fri 0900-1700, Sat-Sun 1000-1400, EU free, €1.60 others*. A series of interesting tombs have been excavated here; belonging to wealthy citizens, they were dug into the rock and crowned with marble or stone structures (none of which survive). You get disinterestedly guided about but can make your way down into many of them, including the massive Tomb of Servilia, daughter of the local governor, where some fragments of wall paintings are conserved. Information is in Spanish and English; try and see the small museum before visiting the site, as it puts the material in context.

Across the road are the remains of an **amphitheatre**. For some shade in Carmona, head for the pretty Alameda near the Paseo.

Ecija

11 buses daily from Prado San Sebastián with
Linesur, 1 hr, 15 mins, €4.87. Map Around Seville

Those with a liking for baroque architecture shouldn't miss this
town east of Seville, although try to get out there early, as the
town is famous for its fearsome summer heat. It's notable for a
series of 18th-century church towers, built at the same period after
the 1755 Lisbon earthquake levelled much of the town. These
towers are cheerfully coloured in bright yellow and blue ceramic
tiles; one of the finest belongs to the **Iglesia de Santa María**
near the main square, **Plaza de España**.

Wandering between churches, you can admire many attractive
façades of palaces built by wealthy landowners. The grandest of
the palaces is the **Palacio de Peñaflor**, built around a patio and
featuring an elaborate staircase topped with a stucco ceiling,
Mon-Fri 1000-1300, 1600-1900; Sat-Sun 1000-1300, free. Another
palace has been converted into a museum displaying Roman finds
(as Astigi, Ecija was an important city) as well as displays of local
culture, including horse breeding, *Tue-Sun 0900-1400; free.*

Jerez de la Frontera

If Seville is a city full of Spanish clichés, Jerez de la Frontera claims
*quite a few of its own. The home of **fancy horses** and **sherry** and a*
*city with a very strong **flamenco tradition**, it's worth a visit if only*
for its markedly different atmosphere to Seville.

Strong ties between Jerez and Britain have been established since
mediaeval times and the love of the island nation for the fortified
wines of this region continues strong. Many of the winemakers and
wine merchants involved in the trade have British roots and certain
things have rubbed off on the locals over the years.

Among the wealthier citizens here you'll spot plenty of tweeds and
spaniels and there's a certain dignified air very different to that found

in other Andalucían cities. That said, there's plenty of Andalucían movida here too.

▶ *See Sleeping p123, Eating and drinking p145*

Nine buses a day (6 at weekends) from Prado San Sebastián bus station between 1230 and 2230, 1 hr, €5.62; 12 trains daily, €5.75, 1hr

 Sights

★ **The town**
Map Around Seville

Recently renovated, Jerez's old centre is an attractive network of palmy plazas and sherry 'n' tapas bars. The main tourist office is on Plaza Arenal, and they'll give you plenty of information on the sights of the city (alternatively, pick up a sheet on Jerez from the tourist kiosk at Seville's Santa Justa station).

If you want to visit a *bodega*, there are several choices. Many go for **González Byass**, home of Tío Pepe, whose pricey tour is a slick affair that won't teach you a lot about sherry making but will let you taste plenty. **Sandeman** is a smaller *bodega* that is recommendable.

It's worth getting to Jerez early so you can head to the **Real Escuela Andaluza de Arte Ecuestre** before lunch and see the highly trained Andalucían horses in side-stepping action, *Tue and Thu from Mar-Oct for the elaborate midday show, €16, and on weekdays when there's no show you can turn up and watch the riders and horses train from 1100-1300, €6.*

The **Alcázar** was the heart of the Moorish town and you can visit the restored Arab baths and mosque. There's also a Renaissance palace here, in which is located a **Camera Obscura**, always a fascinating experience. Opposite is the 18th-century cathedral,

Sherry days
Tío Pepe barrels in Plaza Aladro flanked by Convento Santo Domingo, Jerez de la Frontera.

with a fine Zurbarán Madonna and Child, which is the highlight. Other churches worth a visit are San Miguel, for its elaborately carved portal, and San Marcos, for a fine *retablo*.

Córdoba

*The zenith of Córdoba's influence came in the 10th and 11th centuries when it was the western capital of the Islamic empire, rivalling Baghdad in culture, sophistication and power. Now a large, but insignificant provincial capital, Córdoba preserves plenty of Moorish atmosphere, nowhere more so than in the **Mezquita**, probably the most stunning mosque ever built by the Moors and still an extraordinary place, despite the fact that a Christian cathedral has been built in the middle of it.*

▸▸ *See Sleeping p124, Eating and drinking p146*

10-13 buses daily (roughly hourly on the hour) from Prado de San Sebastián station with Alsina, €8.30 single/€11.80 return; 1hr 45 mins. Six normal trains daily, €6.95, 1hr 20 mins; AVE trains hourly, €19, 41 mins. From the train or bus stations, grab a cab or local bus into the old centre, as it's a fair walk from either.

 Sights

★ La Mezquita
Mon-Sat 1000-1930 (1800 in winter), Sun and festivals 1400-1900 (1800 in winter). Last admission 30 mins before closing. €6.50; under 10s free; 10-14, half price. Enter from C Magistral González Francés. Map 5, F4, p256

Wandering around Córdoba, it's difficult to quite grasp just how large and influential a city this was in Moorish times. Until you enter the Mezquita, that is. The sheer scale of the place, with its never-ending forest of red and white striped arches hits the visitor with some force upon entering from the Patio de los Naranjos, the orange-tree courtyard once used for ritual ablutions. It was begun in AD 785 but built in four distinct phases under different rulers; the last and largest expansion was by the fearsome military tactician Al-Manzur, who brought it to its current size of 23 000 square metres, the size of four football pitches.

It's difficult (and frustrating) to get an idea of what the mosque must once have been like in all its glory, because the conquering Christians decided to park a cathedral in the middle of it. The most drastic alterations took place in 1523 under Carlos V who sanctioned the building, despite local objections, of a chapel and choir in Renaissance style. On inspecting the finished work he did have the decency to comment: *"You have built what you or others might have built anywhere, but you have destroyed something that was unique in the world"*. Don't let that put you off the cathedral, though, which is a fine construction. Among items of particular interest are the mahogany choir stalls, looking like a fantasy of dark chocolate. In the *Tesoro* (Treasury) is a monstrance by Enrique de Arfe, more than 2½ m high, weighing 200 kg and is a mass of jewels, crosses and relics.

Get away from some of the tourists by wandering through the old streets to the east of the Mezquita. Head for the Plaza de la Corredera, a remarkable colonnaded square with several terraced cafés. It was enclosed in the 17th century and formed a multi-purpose arena, which has been used for bullfights and even burnings during the Inquisition.

★ **Judería (Jewish quarter)**
Map 5, C3, p256

Córdoba's *judería*, between the Mezquita and the city walls to the west, is a warren of narrow lanes and alleyways sadly overdosed with souvenir shops. However, you can still find some delightful corners, such as the flower-filled Callejón de las Flores. This street sets the scene for the rest of Córdoba, which takes a great pride in its patios, an architectural remnant from Roman and Moorish times and beautifully decorated, from the humblest home to the grandest palace. The best approach to the *judería* is via the 14th-century Puerta de Almodóvar. From here turn right into Calle Judías, which leads to the Synagogue, one of only three in Spain. Built in 1315, this tiny building has some fine Mudéjar plasterwork of Hebrew texts and retains its women's gallery.

★ The Alcázar

Tue-Sat 1000-1400, 1630-1830, Sun 0930-1430. €2, Fri free.
Gardens open all day Tue-Sun. Map 5, F4, p256

The Alcázar by the river was built by Alfonso X and later enlarged by the Roman Catholic Monarchs. Fernando and Isabel received Columbus in this building before he departed on his first voyage to the New World, while it was also the prison of Boabdil, the last of the kings of Moorish Granada. The Alcázar became a centre for the Inquisition from 1490 until 1821. Even as late as the mid-20th century, the building was functioning as a prison, so it is perhaps not surprising that there is little to see from its golden age. Most enjoyable is wandering around the gardens to the south of the building, with its pools, fountains and rose beds, which are illuminated during the summer evenings.

With dozens of hotels set in attractively renovated old Seville mansions, there's a wealth of choice of attractive, intimate lodgings in the city. Accommodation is classified into hotels and *hostales* with star ratings, but these aren't necessarily a good guide to either quality or price; there are plenty of one-star hotels with superb facilities, and several *hostales* that charge hotel-like prices. The densest concentration of accommodation can be found in Barrio Santa Cruz and San Vicente between the Plaza de Armas bus station and the Museo de Bellas Artes. If you're planning a visit in spring, booking ahead is advisable, although there are enough options that you'll never have to sleep on the street. All places raise their prices during Semana Santa and Feria; this increase can be double or more, although it's more commonly 50-70%. At some hotels, this increase is in place for the whole March-May period. At this time, look out for people at the bus/train station offering rooms in private homes; these can be a good deal. Seville's accommodation is expensive by Spanish standards;

Price

Sleeping codes

LL	€150 +	C	€45-60
L	€120-150	D	€38-45
AL	€100-120	E	€30-38
A	€80-100	F	€20-30
B	€60-80	G	€20 or under

The following codes are used to indicate prices. Prices are inclusive of IVA (VAT) and represent the cost of a double room in high season, but not during Semana Santa or Feria, when a room typically costs 50-70% more.

the cheapest period is in winter, but many places also drop their prices in July and August, when the weather is unbearable and there's nobody in town. Self-catering is another option; there are many apartments available for short-term rent in good locations and they tend to be well-priced compared to a hotel or *hostal* of the same standard.

The cathedral and around

Hotels and hostales

LL Hotel Seises, C Segovias 6, **T** 954 229 495, **F** 954 224 334, seises@jet.es *Map 2, D4, p250* Attractive, 16th-century *palacio* converted into a modern hotel. It's good, peaceful and comfortable with relaxed, friendly service. There's a big lounge and garden, but the highlight is the rooftop terrace and pool with the Giralda looming a stone's throw away. Rooms are modern and stylish but not cheap.

L Hotel Doña María, C Don Remondo 19, **T** 954 224 990,
F 954 219 546, www.hdmaria.com *Map 2, D4, p250* This fairly
plush hotel is right by the cathedral. Despite the rather heavy
decor of the public areas the rooms are spacious and comfortable
with slightly twee, pinky-red fittings and most conveniences.
Service is classically courteous. Limited parking available at a price.

A Hospedería Dalí, Puerta de Jerez 3, **T** 954 220 595,
hdali@arrakis.es *Map 2, I3, p251* The newly opened Dalí is
on the busy Puerta de Jerez roundabout, but it's not as noisy as
you'd expect. The rooms all have ample balconies and are bright
and attractive, with refurbished wooden cornicing. The lobby
features bright floral paintings.

A Hotel Zurbarán, C Mariana de Pineda 10, **T** 954 210 646,
hzurbaran@arrakis.es *Map 2, H4, p251* This charming hotel is
set around a high lobby filled with hanging plants and sun and
moon mirrors. The service is friendly and the big rooms feature
sofas and attractive wrought-iron headboards. The overall
atmosphere is tranquil and relaxing.

B Hostal Van Gogh, C Miguel de Mañara 4, **T/F** 954 563 727,
hvangogh@arrakis.es *Map 2, G3, p251* A friendly, attractive place,
one of four co-owned "painters" hotels in this quiet corner of old
Seville. The main noise to be heard is the odd horse carriage
clopping by. The rooms are welcoming, with some original wooden
cornicing, small bathrooms and some geraniumed balconies.

B Nuevo Hostal Picasso, C San Gregorio 1, **T** 954 210 864,
hpicasso@arrakis.es *Map 2, I3, p251* Another very pleasant
offering from the "painters quartet", the Picasso is serene and
friendly, in a renovated Sevillan house near the Alcázar and
cathedral. The tiled lobby is shaded with ferns and the rooms are
comfortable with pretty bedsteads and a soothing colour scheme.

B YH Giralda, C Abades 30, **T** 954 228 324, www.yh-hoteles.com
Map 2, D5, p250 Not to be confused with a youth hostel, this
minimalist marble-decorated hotel has a superb location in a
quiet street. There's good service and the rooms are elegant,
comfortable and cool.

D Hostal Arias, C Mariana de Pineda 9, **T** 954226840, **F** 954 218
389, www.hostalarias.com *Map 2, H4, p251* Location is the key
here, tucked into a quiet alley a couple of hundred crooked metres
from the cathedral. The rooms are bright and cheery – a few have
tiny balconies. It's good value except in high season.

D Pensión Alcázar, C Deán Miranda 12, **T** 954 228 457. *Map 2,
H4, p251* This *pensión* has simple and pleasant spacious rooms
with tiled floors, some with miniature ensuite bathrooms. There's
a sunny terrace for guests to use, as well as another for use of the
"penthouse" room, which is slightly more expensive.

Barrio Santa Cruz

Hotels and hostales

LL Hotel Fernando III, C San José 21, **T** 954 217 307,
F 954 220 246, fernandoiii@altur.com *Map 2, E6, p250*
This central hotel is big and light. Although the lobby and lounge
have a sterile feel, the rooms are nice, with wooden bedheads and
excellent bathrooms. The rooftop pool is a bonus.

LL Hotel Rey Alfonso X, C Ximénez de Enciso 35, **T** 954 210 070,
F 954 220 246, www.reyalfonsox.com *Map 2, E6, p250* This
modern hotel is big, large, light and quite sleek with plenty of glass
panels. The rooms feature big, comfortable beds and some have
views over the busy *terrazas* of Calle Santa María la Blanca.

★ **Hotels with luxury and charm**

Sleeping

LL **Las Casas de la Judería**, Cjón Dos Hermanas 7, **T** 954 415 150, **F** 954 422 170, www.casasypalacios.com *Map 2, D7, p250*
This spreads across several old *palacios* – all have been renovated with sparkling patios, pretty nooks, and hanging foliage. The rooms are large, luxurious enough and pleasant, though not a patch on the exterior decor and a little dark and stuffy. There's live music in the piano bar every evening. A particular highlight is the originally decorated underground passageway to the dining room.

A **Hotel Amadeus**, C Farnesio 6, **T** 954 501 443, **F** 954 500 019, www.hotelamadeussevilla.com *Map 2, E6, p250* A fantastic and original small hotel with a musical theme. The rooms are all named after composers; some have a piano in them. Some of the rooms are fabulous, some merely excellent; all have good facilities. A highlight, apart from the friendly service, is the spacious roof terrace with views around the centre, including the Giralda. Highly recommended.

A **Hotel Puerta de Sevilla**, C Puerta de la Carne 2 (formerly the end of C Santa María la Blanca), **T** 954 987 270, **F** 954 987 360, www.hotelpuertadesevilla.com *Map 2, F7, p250* Opened in April 2003, this pleasant hotel has colourful, flowery rooms with good, modern bathrooms and the expected conveniences. There's disabled access, pleasant service, and a nice little lounge with a pretty tiled fountain burbling away. Handy for public transport and there's underground parking close by.

B Hostería de Doña Lina, C Gloria 7, **T** 954 210 956,
F 954 218 661, www.hlina.com *Map 2, G5, p251* A good-value
accommodation choice above a friendly restaurant. There's some
nice tilework around the stairs and corridors; the rooms themselves
are slightly careworn, but it's not a bad price for the location.

B Hostal Goya, C Mateos Gago 31, **T** 954 211 170, **F** 954 562 988.
Map 2, E5, p250 Located at the top of the street in Seville's tapas
epicentre, it's a dark, cool place with marbled floors and a/c, a
welcome retreat after a few *manzanillas* in the scorching sun.
Unusually, Semana Santa prices are scarcely higher than normal.

C Hostal Córdoba, C Farnesio 12, **T** 954 227 498. *Map 2, E6,
p250* Clean, modernized, and friendly, this makes a good, if
slightly pricey base on a small street. The rooms are very pleasant,
light, and quiet and the bathrooms are modern and very clean.
The hostal's patio is brightly tiled with coppery colours.

D Hostal Dulces Sueños/Sweet Dreams, C Santa María la
Blanca 21 (now called Puerta de la Carne), **T** 954 419 393. *Map 2,
F8, p250* A good little option with a variety of modern rooms,
with or without bath. It's spotless; the rooms are nice, light and
comfy and have good, firm beds, tiled floors and, crucially for this
category, air-conditioning. Friendly and handy.

D Hostal Pérez Montilla, Pl de Curtidores 13, **T** 954 421 854,
perezmontilla@hotmail.com *Map 2, E7, p250* A clean, friendly
choice in a less-touristed section of the Barrio Santa Cruz. Most
of the rooms are light and comfortable with good bathroom.
There are also some cheap, if simple, single rooms available.

D Hostal San Francisco, C González de León 4, **T** 954 536 876.
Map 2, D8, p250 A family run place that makes a pretty good
option. The patio is very nicely decorated with blue tiles and the

rooms are good, with colourful bedspreads and curtains and bathroom. There's a little noise from the nearby main road, but not too much, and the place is spotless.

E Hostal Buen Dormir/Good Sleep, C Farnesio 8, **T** 954 217 492. *Map 2, E6, p250* A well-priced option with small, but colourful, comfy rooms set around a nice patio filled with the chirruping of caged birds. Some rooms come with small bathrooms, the others with shower. Laundry service available.

E Pensión Vergara, C Ximénez de Enciso 11, **T** 954 215 668. *Map 2, E6, p250* This budget option is set around a pleasant patio in a restored 15th-century house. There's a room for 12 people, who pay €18 each – and singles, doubles or shared options. The entrance is shared with a shop next to the Casa Plácido tapas bar.

F Hostal San Pancracio, Plaza de las Cruces 9, **T** 954 413 104, pensionsanpancracio@hotmail.com *Map 2, F7, p250* In a quiet nook of the barrio, this is a sound, cheap choice, a touch faded, but clean and quiet. There are several room choices: they are all adequate, with attractive, white calico bedspreads and light and air from a central patio.

F Hostal Santa María La Blanca, C Santa María la Blanca 28, **T** 954 421 174. *Map 2, F7, p250* Rooms are simple but prettily tiled and have a much-needed fan. The upstairs ones, with bathroom, are nicer, with more light available. Service here is friendly and the price is good.

Self-catering

Apartamentos Murillo, C Reinoso 6, **T** 954 210 959, **F** 954 219 616, www.hotelmurillo.com/apartamentos *Map 2, F5, p250* Good apartments run by the hotel of the same name. There are two types, sleeping three or five, and fitted out with kitchen, bathroom, TV and phone. Rates are good for this location, at €390 a week for the smaller apartment.

Apartamentos Santa Cruz, Pl de los Venerables s/n, **T** 954 223 583, **F** 954 563 806, www.sevilla.net/a-santacruz *Map 2, F5, p250* Good apartments and although not huge, are well-equipped and priced at €97 per day, with discounts for longer stays. Kitchen includes a microwave and some apartments have their own terrace.

South of the cathedral

Hotels and hostales

LL **Alfonso XIII**, C San Fernando 2, **T** 954 917 000, **F** 954 917 099, www.hotel-alfonsoxiii.com *Map 2, I3, p251* One of Spain's most luxurious hotels, this huge, neo-Moorish building was erected for the 1929 exhibition. Beautifully decorated with opulent patios, the hotel is five star in every sense of the word, but the prices are exorbitant at nearly €500 for a double and more during Seville's festive season.

El Arenal

Hotels and hostales

LL **Hotel La Rábida**, C Castelar 24, **T** 954 220 960, **F** 954 224 375, www.vinccihoteles.com *Check web for special offers.* *Map 2, E1, p250* This hotel is far more beautifully decorated and appointed than you normally expect from a chain establishment. With a façade of red ochre, the rooms are built around an attractive galleried atrium with a fountain. They're comfortable and stylish, with large firm beds and modern bathrooms, as well as internet connection point and video games.

A **Hotel Maestranza**, C Gamazo 12, **T** 954 561 070, **F** 954 214 404, www.hotel-maestranza.com   *Map 2, E1, p250* An attractive hotel in a good location handy for the Arenal tapas bars. Painted up in soft ochre tones with hanging pictures and coppery tiles, the decor exudes Seville, almost to excess. Service is friendly and the rooms are spacious with decent bathroom.

B **Hotel Simón**, C García de Vinuesa 19, **T** 954 226 660, **F** 954 562 241, www.hotelsimonsevilla.com   *Map 2, E2, p250* Very attractive hotel built around a beautiful, airy courtyard with a fountain. There are plenty of *azulejos* and neo-Moorish features. Rooms are smallish but welcoming. Very well priced for the decor and ambience.

Triana

Hotels and hostales

E **Hostal Guadalquivir**, Pagés del Corro 53, **T** 954 332 100, **F** 954 332 104.   *Map 3, H3, p253* Good option across the river in Triana. There's nice tiling although some of the decor is a little heavier. Rooms are well-priced and come with or without bath; those at the front can be a little noisy.

Centro and San Vicente

Hotels and hostales

LL **Hotel Casa Imperial**, C Imperial 29, **T** 954 500 300, **F** 954 500 330, www.casaimperial.com   *Map 2, B7, p250* This elegant *palacio* is one of Seville's most luxurious accommodation options. The rooms are all suites with individual decor based on Moorish or Andalucían themes. They are seriously comfortable, have either balcony or patio, and have an elegance that is relaxing rather than starchy. Service is top-notch, a good breakfast is included in the price, and the patios are enchanting.

L Hotel Inglaterra, Pl Nueva 7, **T** 954 224 970, **F** 954 561 336, www.hotelinglaterra.es *Map 2, C1, p250* With its trademark London cab sitting out the front, this hotel is something of a Seville emblem; in fact, it was shelled by Queipo de Llano during the early days of the 1936 military coup as it was sheltering some loyalist troops. Not too many leftist associations remain however: Hackney carriage and Irish bar aside, it's a fairly formal Spanish hotel with heavy, elegant decor and polite service.

L Las Casas de los Mercaderes, C Alvarez Quintero 9, **T** 954 225 858, **F** 954 229 884, www.casasypalacios.com *Map 2, C3, p250* A beautifully renovated hotel, sibling establishment to Las Casas de la Judería (see p114). The rooms are attractively furnished and spacious, with all conveniences; the hotel is built around a beautiful arcaded patio. Elegant, 19th-century furnishings in the public areas complete the classy but welcoming feeling.

L Las Casas del Rey de Baeza, Pl Jesús de la Redención 2, off Calle Santiago, **T** 954 561 496, **F** 954 561 441, www.hospes.es *Map 2, A7, p250* An enchanting place to stay near Casa Pilatos, this old *corral de vecinos* has been superbly restored to be charming, but not overdone. The patios are surrounded by pretty wooden galleries. The rooms are big with huge beds and all facilities. Guests have use of a rooftop pool and terrace as well as a beautifully decorated library and lounges. The service is excellent and the price very low for this quality. Highly recommended.

A Hotel Baco, Pl Ponce de León 15, **T** 954 565 050, **F** 954 563 654. *Map 4, L7, p255* Attractively decorated with tiles, green leather chairs and dark wood. The rooms all have minibar, phone and a/c. Those on the street are double-glazed, but they're all well-fitted, light and airy and the staff are courteous. Underground parking is available and there's a good cod tapas bar downstairs.

A Hotel Puerta de Triana, C Reyes Católicos 5, **T** 954 215 404, **F** 954 215 401, www.hotelpuertadetriana.com *Map 3, D7, p252*
This smart and friendly hotel puts to shame a lot of its brethren that charge double the price. It's spotless, comfortable and decorated in marble veneer and attractive rugs. The rooms are great – some open onto a quiet, leafy interior patio; they have all facilities. Breakfast is included in the price. Recommended.

B Hotel Doña Blanca, Plaza Jerónimo de Córdoba, **T** 954 501 373, **F** 954 216 443, hdonablanca@inicia.es *Map 4, L8, p255* In an attract ively renovated red ochre building, this small hotel offers plenty of good-value comfort. The beds are firm and welcoming and some of the rooms have balconies from which you may hear strains of Pepe Peregil singing from his bar across the square. There's a nice atrium-lounge and attractive cane and *espartero* fittings.

C Hotel Zaida, C San Roque 26, **T** 954 213 612, **F** 954 218 810, hzaida26@hotmail.com *Map 3, B8, p252* The neo-Moorish patio is the nicest part about this hotel. The rooms aren't as good with fairly small beds and bathrooms – some are better than others, so shop around. Management is relaxed and friendly and if other places are full you can do a lot worse.

E Hostal El Giraldillo, C Gravina 23, **T** 954 224 275. *Map 2, C8, p250* Another decent option on this little street, the Giraldillo has likeable management and small, white rooms around a narrow central atrium. Although most of the bathrooms are exterior, they are private to the rooms. The owners will let you in at all hours without a murmur, but their sleepy faces might prompt compass-ionate party animals to stay elsewhere. Handy for the bus station.

E Pensión Virgen de la Luz, C Virgen de la Luz 18, **T** 954 537 963. *Map 2, C8, p250* One of Seville's best-value cheapies, this pretty little place is near the Casa de Pilatos. The rooms come with or without bath; the latter are of an unusually high standard and represent good value, particularly those on the lane, which have a small balcony full of plants. The beds are welcoming, the bathroom spotless, and the patio decorated nicely with blue tiling.

F Hostal Bailén, C Bailén 75, **T** 954 221 635. *Map 3, A7, p252* There are prettier *pensiones* around, but there's something very nice about this cheapie at the back of the Museo de Bellas Artes. From the empty champagne and whisky bottles in a display case to the serious 10 year old that shows you the rooms, to the *simpatico* management, it's full of character. The rooms vary, but most are simple and charming and there are a couple of excellent ones, such as numbers 2 and 5. They're well-priced, even in Semana Santa, and there are also apartments for rent down the road. Recommended.

F Hostal Romero, C Gravina 21, **T** 954 211 353. *Map 3, A6, p252* A friendly little *pensión* run by a sympathetic family. The rooms have a simple charm but can be a bit stuffy in summer. There's a very nice, light patio and some attractive furniture around the place. Rooms without bath are a better deal than those with bath, unless you can score room 5, which has access to another small space filled with greenery.

Self-catering

Sevilla Apartamentos, **T** 667 511 348, www.sevillapartamentos. com This organization has a range of good apartments for short-term rental in different areas. Prices are around €240 for two people for a week, which represents very good value. You can examine photos and rates on the website.

Alojamientos Sevilla, T 696 432 253, **F** 954 229 269, www.alojamientos-sevilla.com An agency with several good apartments around Seville available for rental for periods of 3 days and longer. Returnable deposit of € 200 payable.

La Macarena

Hotels and hostales

A **Patio de la Cartuja and Patio de la Alameda**, C Lumbreras 8 & Alameda de Hércules 56, **T** 954 900 200, **F** 954 902 056, www.patiosdesevilla.com *Map 4, F3, p254* These beautiful apart-hotels make top value places to stay. Both are built around beautiful, orange, restored patios and have excellent rooms with sitting room, kitchen and all facilities. Both offer equally high standards and the same prices; the Cartuja is marginally nicer, on a quieter street, and with a beautiful long patio. Recommended.

D **Hostal Muralla**, C Fray Diego de Cádiz 39, **T** 954 371 049, **F** 954 379 411, hmuralla@terra.es *Map 4, E7, p254* A good, quiet option in the shadow of the Moorish walls. It's clean, colourful, quiet and friendly; the rooms with balcony are the nicest; the others can be a trifle stuffy, although all rooms have a/c. There are cold drinks available in the foyer and parking is relatively easy in this corner of old Seville.

E **Hostal Macarena**, C San Luís 91, **T** 954 370 141. *Map 4, E6, p254* Excellent option on the Plaza del Pumarejo, family run and set around a lovely light atrium. The tilework is beautiful, and there's some attractive and original furniture. Bright, friendly and very clean. Rooms with or without bath available.

Carmona

Hotels and hostales

LL **Casa de Carmona**, Plaza de Lasso 1, **T** 954 191 000, **F** 954 190 189, www.casadecarmona.com A superbly restored *palacio* in the heart of Carmona's old town, this is furnished in period style, has very comfortable rooms, a top restaurant and a swimming pool – a godsend in this sunbeaten town.

AL **Parador del Rey Don Pedro**, C Los Alcázares s/n, **T** 954 141 010, **F** 954 141 712, www.parador.es The upper Alcázar, once used as a palace by the charismatic Pedro I, has been partially restored to house this, one of southern Spain's finest *paradors*. There are great views over the town and the plains below.

D **Pensión Comercio**, C Torre del Oro 56, **T** 954 140 018. Right next to the impressive Puerta de Seville and tucked inside the walls, this is a spruce option which is pretty good value for a stay in Carmona. It's air-conditioned, has a pretty patio, good management and a cheap restaurant.

Jerez de la Frontera

Hotels and hostales

C **Trujillo**, C Medina 36, **T** 956 342 438.   An unusual and characterful hotel in an 18th-century mansion with neo-Moorish wooden ceilings. Faded but pleasing rooms; plenty of character and significantly cheaper off-season (**E**).

E San Andrés, C Morenos 12, **T** 956 340 983.   This is a delightful place to stay with balconied rooms, a beautiful tiled tropical coutryard and garden that is the owner's pride and joy. An excellent option in this price range. Recommended.

Córdoba

Hotels and hostales

AL Posada de Vallina, C Corregidor Luís de la Cerda 83, **T** 957 498 750, **F** 957 498 751, hotel@hotelvallina.com *Map 5, E6, p256* A small, newish hotel and restaurant across from the Mezquita, the building is magnificent with Roman columns and an ancient well. The 15 rooms are decorated in contemporary Andalucían style with small balconies.

C Maestre, C Romero Barros 4, **T** 957 472 410, **F** 957 475 395. *Map 5, C8, p256* A well-located quiet hostal near the Plaza del Potro with traditionally furnished rooms around an attractive patio. Very good value and friendly management.

F Hostal Plaza Corredera, Plaza Corredera 1, **T** 957 470 581. *Map 5, A8, p256* Friendly, refurbished place with good rooms looking out over the pretty plaza. Whitewashed and rambling with a very low price. Recommended.

Despite the beautiful Alcázar, the lofty cathedral and the wealth of inspired art, your best moments in Seville are likely to be spent eating. Tapas was invented here and it's the place in Spain that it is done best. In reality, there's little distinction between restaurants and tapas bars in Seville; most of the former include an area to stand and snack, while at the latter you can usually sit down and order *raciones* (meal-sized portions). Accepted practice is to stand at the bar, have at most a couple of tapas in each, and have a taste of what your friends are eating. A standard tapa will cost €1-2.

Another Spanish institution is the *menú del día*, a filling, set price three-course meal offered at lunchtime (1330-1530 roughly). These normally cost €5-10 but will be more (and usually poorer value) in more expensive restaurants.

On the tapas crawl, people tend to drink wine or beer. Spanish lager is good, particularly *Cruzcampo*; and you should at least try the local *finos* and *manzanillas*, dry sherries that don't appeal to all palates but are a great accompaniment to seafood.

€ Eating codes

€€€ € 30 and over
€€ € 15-30
€ € 15 and under

Prices refer to a two course meal for one excluding drinks.

The cathedral and around

Restaurants

€€ **Monriot**, C Don Remondo 1, **T** 954 211 731. *Tue-Sun 1100-2400*. *Map 2, E4, p250* A likeable restaurant in the quiet backstreets near the cathedral. The interior features attractive brick walls and bishop's mitre seats as well as some Arabic lettering here and there. The chef's not afraid to experiment a little on Andalucían themes and the various stew-type dishes here are toothsome.

€€ **Robles Placentines**, C Placentines 2, **T** 954 213 162. *1200-0130*. *Map 2, E4, p250* Poor service lets down this attractive restaurant which has lovely outdoor tables. Notwithstanding, they do some decent fish dishes and the wine selection is good. At the bar, try the *brochetas de pescado* (fish kebabs) or the slightly strange smoked salmon in a sweet sauce.

Tapas bars

Bodega El Cortijo, C Alvarez Quintero 60. **T** 954 227 539. *1200-1600, 1900-0100*. *Map 2, E3, p250* Very simple and friendly bar in the shadow of the cathedral that couldn't be more authentic. Not a frill in sight, just tasty *montaditos* served until late and an untouristy crowd spilling onto the street.

Bar Gonzalo, C Alemanes 21, **T** 954 223 595. *0700-0300. Map 2, E3, p250* Although it's just by the cathedral and thus in prime tourist zone, this is a good tapas option with some good fishy bites including *calamares en su tinta* and some very fat tortilla and *empanada*. The restaurant's speciality is seafood.

Cafés

Picalagartos, C Hernando Colón 5, **T** 954 226 940. *1600-0230. Map 2, D3, p250* A decent café with Portuguese-style tiles and a pretty, worked ceiling. Upstairs is the best spot to lurk with a coffee; it's nice and cosy and decorated with photos of Central America.

Barrio Santa Cruz

Restaurants

€€€€ **La Albahaca**, Pl Santa Cruz 12, **T** 954 220 714. *Mon-Sat 1200-1600, 2000-2400. Map 2, F6, p250* Set in a lovely mansion, this is one of the city's finest restaurants. There's a fine little terrace, but the interior is also attractive, with replica paintings and *comme-il-faut* service. The food's classy with a distinct French influence. Dishes worthy of the surrounds include oysters au gratin with dill and *cava*, pheasant salad or wild boar well matched with a fig and orange compôte.

€€ **Corral del Agua**, Cjón del Agua 6, **T** 954 220 714. *Mon-Sat 1200-1600, 2000-2400. Map 2, G6, p251* A top spot to escape the narrow streets, this restaurant is lucky enough to have an enclosed terrace right by the Almohad walls. It's touristy, but classy, and serves up great Seville specialities like *huevos a la flamenca* as well as several fine salmon options.

€€ **Coello**, C Doncellas 8. *Map 2, E7, p250* This elegant, backstreet restaurant doesn't seem to pull many tourists in, but there's no reason why not. The furnishing is light and stylish and there's a very attractive terrace. The food is freshly prepared and includes good fish and meat dishes and tasty salads and sangria. There's a *menú del día* for €9.10 which is very good value.

Tapas bars

Abacería Puerta Carmona, C Puerta Carmona 38, **T** 954 420 695. *1200-2400. Map 2, E5, p250* A characterful and friendly place with wooden floors, this bar has a mini second floor with acres of sherry and serves excellent tapas in an authentic atmosphere. There's a big selection of goat and sheep cheeses and cured meats in particular.

Bar Alfalfa, corner C Alfalfa & C Candilejo, **T** 954 213 354. *1100-0100. Map 2, B5, p250* Decorated with farming implements, earthenware jars, and hundreds of bottles of wine, you can enjoy a perfect *bruschetta* here or a selection of Italian cheeses. Spills outside on warm evenings.

Bar Campanario, C Mateos Gago 8, **T** 954 564 189. *1200-2400 (0100 in summer). Map 2, F4, p250* An attractive option with warm staff and a good range of vegetarian salads and snacks as well as meatier fare. Try the *gratinado de berenjenas* while sitting on the small terrace.

Bar Las Teresas, C Santa Teresa 2, **T** 954 213 069. *Mon-Fri 0900-2400, Sat 1000-0200, Sun 1100-2400. Map 2, F6, p250* With a handful of outdoor tables, this bar obviously sees plenty of passing tourist traffic, but it's worth a stop. Decorated with bullfight scenes and hanging hams, the cured meats are good and served with spuds if you like.

Bar Patanchón, C Mateos Gago 13, **T** 954 224 708. *1200-0200. Map 2, E5, p250* While it's only halves and *raciones* on the terrace here, head inside for some unusual and delicious tapas – the camembert in raspberry sauce is particularly noteworthy.

Bodega Santa Cruz, C Rodrigo Caro 2. *1200-2400. Map 2, E5, p250* This is a busy and cheerful bar, largely because it does some of Seville's choicest tapas and *montaditos*. Sees plenty of tourists but still very authentic close to the Giralda. Highly recommended.

Carmela, C Santa María la Blanca 6. *Map 2, E7, p250* One of the better of the terraced bars on this long plaza, Carmela serves food all day from 0900. There are good breakfasts, plenty of vegetarian dishes and snacks, and decent tapas, as well as a *plato del día* that's good value for this part of town at €6.

Casa Plácido, C Mesón del Moro 5, **T** 954 563 971. *Mon-Thu 1200-1600, 2000-2400, Fri-Sun 1200-0100. Map 2, E5, p250* A likeable place in the warren-like centre of the barrio, but comparatively untouristed. Staff are friendly and serve up a variety of good stuff in the bullfight-decorated interior or on the small terrace. Good choices include the tasty sausages, or dates with bacon.

Casa Roman, Pl de los Venerables 1, **T** 954 228 483. *0900-1600, 1700-0030. Map 2, F5, p250* A little over-touristy but still deservedly popular with locals, this bar serves up excellent, well-priced *jamón*, full of big flavour. There are also some good meat dishes and a couple of tasty *revueltos* – try the one *con ajetes* (garlic shoots).

Casa Sergio, C Lope de Rueda 18, **T** 954 215 435. *Map 2, F6, p250* This no-frills tapas bar draws a loyal local crowd including a few painters whose canvases adorn the walls. The service can be slow, but the tapas are good – try the *huevos de codorniz* (quails' eggs) or the salty *riñones al jerez* (kidneys cooked in sherry).

La Giralda, C Mateos Gago 1, **T** 954 227 435. *0900-2400*. *Map 2, E4, p250* Despite the fact the bar staff occasionally find it amusing to overcharge tourists, this tapas bar is one of Seville's better ones, for the size and quality of the portions. The decor is attractive with pretty tiles and a Moorish feel. Particularly recommended is the *solomillo*.

La Goleta, C Mateos Gago. *Tue-Sun 0900-1500, 2000-2300*. *Map 2, E5, p250* Tiny bar with loads of character. Run by the son of Pepe Peregil (see Bar Quita Pesares, p153), who is a chip off the old block, it's been in the family since 1941. It specializes in a tasty orange wine; the tapas are limited but excellent, particularly the "candid" tortilla.

Cafés

Alfalfa 10, Plaza Alfalfa 10, **T** 954 213 841. *0900-0100*. *Map 2, B5, p250* A bar-café whose main virtue is a range of absolutely delicious cakes baked by the German owner. Cheesecake like it's meant to be, *sachertorte*, *kirschtorte*, it's all here...

South of the cathedral

Restaurants

€€€ **Egaña Oriza**, C San Fernando 41, **T** 954 227 211.*1330-1600, 2100-2400*. *Map 2, I5, p251* A smart restaurant with a noted chef who blends Andalucían cuisine with his native Basque styles. The pavilion-style room has attractive and comfortable white furniture; things that are done particularly well are *salmorejo*, stewed wood-pigeon, sole with saffron sauce and a great *ceviche* of monkfish and grouper. There's also a tapas bar which is *pijo* but has some tasty salads and canapés.

Tapas bars

Bar Hermanos Gómez, Jardines Murillo s/n, **T** 954 211 926. *Map 2, I5, p251* One of a few branches, this *chiringuito* by the gardens should be tried for its delicious prawns. Six of the things and a glass of cold house red will set you back €2 and breathe new life into a garlic-drenched palate.

Cafés

Chile, Av de las Delicias s/n, **T** 954 235 258. *0900-0400*. *Map 2, L4, p251* A cool, yellow bar, popular with students from the nearby faculties. It's in the quiet heart of the 1929 exhibition area, and has a pleasant, leafy terrace. Frequent live music at weekends.

El Arenal

Restaurants

€€ **As-Sawirah**, C Galera 5, **T** 954 562 268. *1200-1600, 2100-2400*. *Map 3, E7, p252* A stylish Moroccan restaurant in a hidden backstreet. Good service and a small but authentic range of high-quality cuisine, including *tajines*, cous-cous, and an excellent Berber salad with goats cheese.

€€ **El Buzo**, C Antonia Díaz 5, **T** 954 210 231. *1100-0100, Fri-Sat 1100 -0200*. *Map 2, F1, p250* A busy and happy restaurant, decorated with pictures of bullfighters and hanging lamps. The *raciones* are excellent; particularly the *solomillo al whisky*.

€€ **Restaurante Puerta Grande**, C Antonia Díaz 33, **T** 954 216 843. *Map 3, H8, p253* Opposite the bullring, this smart eatery is predictably decorated with *trajes de luz* (matadors' suits). There's good dining to be done here; the *solomillo* is a house specialty, there's a variety of seafood, and the *revueltos* are also excellent.

€ **Café-Bar Veracruz**, Paseo de las Delicias 1, **T** 954 225 315. *0800-0100*. *Map 2, I2, p251* Unfashionable, no-frills joint with plastic terrace enjoying views of the Torre del Oro. The staff are friendly, the tapas good and there's an €8.50 *menú*.

€ **Casa de Postas**, C Reyes Católicos 25, **T** 954 563 479. *1230-0100*. *Map 2, E6, p251* Ignoring the pre-fab paella menus, this tiny bar offers some great food on its terrace (20% price hike for the privilege). Recommended options include *espinacas con garbanzos* (spinach with chickpeas), good grilled meats, and tasty *migas*.

€ **Infanta Sevilla**, C Arfe 36, **T** 954 229 689. *Tue-Sun 0900-1700, 2000-0100*. *Map 2, G1, p251* A popular, smartly decorated bar which has exceptionally well-priced food. The warm decoration is typically Spanish, full of bottles, barrels and hanging joints of ham; the *raciones* cost €5-€8; try *hojaldre relleno de buey*, the house rice, or *tortilla al whisky*.

Tapas bars

Antigua Abacería de San Lorenzo, C Arfe s/n. *Tue-Sun 0830-2400*. *Map 2, F2, p250* A cosy little bar that was once a grocers and still has the old wooden floors and deli products on the shelves. The place smells of strong cheese; the tapas here are good; it's also a decent spot for breakfast.

Arena, C Adriano 10, **T** 954 219 364. *1200-0100 (0400 at weekends)*. *Map 2, F1, p250* A cool bar, the tapas here are "*artesanas*" and there's certainly a variety on offer. The *salmorejo* is excellent, there are good vegetarian options and some tasty cakes, all eagerly consumed by a trendy, youngish set.

★ **Generous tapas**

• A *solomillo al whisky* at Bodegón Don Julián, p139
• *Habas con jamón* at the Faro de Triana, p137
• A *pincho de pollo* at Bodega Santa Cruz, p130
• A *carrillada* at Nueva Enramadilla, p144
• A *caldereta de venao* at Bar Pepe Hillo, p134

Bar Pepe Hillo, C Adriano 24, **T** 954 215 390. *1200-0100. Map 3, F8, p252* A legend in its own tapas time, especially for stews such as the *caldereta de venao* venison dish and some very tasty *croquetas* among other goodies. High-ceilinged, busy and buzzy, it's decorated with farming implements and has a small, popular terrace.

Bodegas Díaz-Salazar, C García de Vinuesa 18, **T** 954 213 181. *1130-1600, 1900-0030. Closed Sun evening. Map 2, E2, p250* It doesn't get much more authentic. This spacious century-old *bodega* has faded posters, an ageing clientele, and top sherries drawn from the barrel. The bar staff dress in old green sweaters and keep the chalk for reckonings behind their ears. The *montaditos* and limited tapas are simple and good.

Casa Morales, C García de Vinuesa 11, **T** 954 221 242. *Mon-Sat 1200-1600, 2000-0130. Map 2, E2, p250* This great old place is in an old sherry *bodega*. The service is old-style, with chalk on the bar and friendly chat. The tapas and *montaditos* are served on a wee wooden tray; the *guiso del día* (stew of the day) is often a tempting option.

Cafés

Bengué, C Postigo del Carbón 6. *1000-0100. Map 2, H1, p251* An attractive, modern café – a good spot for coffee, but don't linger too long as the furniture is designed for looks rather than comfort.

Triana

Restaurants

€€ **El Candil**, C Paraíso 3, **T** 954 274 784. *1200-1700, 2000-0100.*
Map 3, L6, p253   A popular tapas and lunch spot, this is a pleasantly-
lit restaurant with wooden beams and tiled pictures of old Seville.
The service is a highlight, as are the fish dishes – try *urta*, a kind of
bream. The *solomillo* in cheese sauce is also a cracker.

€€ **La Triana**, C Castilla 36, **T** 954 333 819. *Tue-Sun 1300-1630,
2030-0030.   Map 3, E2, p252*   A light and modern place with some
river views, this place serves up some seriously good food with
contemporary innovation taking its place alongside some traditional
Andalucían fare. Try turkey rolls stuffed with chard and red pepper
sauce (*rollitos de pavo rellenos de acelga*).

€€ **La Vega de Triana**, Pl San Martín de Porres 4, **T** 954 337
144.   *Map 3, K1, p253*   A well-decorated place with tiled pictures
and drinkers eating tapas off barrels. The menu is strong on
chargrilled meats; also an extensive choice of fried fish and *panes*.

€€ **Samurai**, C Salado 6, **T** 954 283 106.   *Map 3, L7, p253*
A peaceful backstreet Japanese restaurant which has a good lunch
special for €5.81 on weekdays. The food and service are good, and
the wooden furnishing elegant and relaxing. Makes a good change
from Andalucían food if you're looking for one.

€ **Cervecería La Mar**, Av de Coria 5, **T** 954 343 930. *1200-1600,
1900-0000.   Map 3, K1, p253*   A big barn of a place run by Mariscos
Emilio whose tasty seafood pops up in a number of places around
the city. It's basically a place to eat prawns and drink beer; a big plate
of the former and a litre of the latter will set you back just € 8.10.

★ Unusual eats

Best

- Camembert with raspberry sauce at Bar Patanchón, p130
- Partridge paté at Bar Europa, p139
- Grouper meatballs at Yebra, p142
- Fish roe salad at La Primera del Puente, p136

€ **La Primera del Puente**, C Betis 66, **T** 954 276 918. *1100-1700, 1930-0030. Closed Wed. Map 3, K8, p253* Despite its excellent location on the river, this is a fairly cheap place. The terrace faces the Torre del Oro and the average *ración* costs €8. While it's far from subtle, the food is good; there's a tapas bar too, decorated with tiled pictures of the river. Recommended.

Tapas bars

Blanca Paloma, C Pagés del Corro 86, **T** 954 333 788. *0800-1600, 2000-2400. Map 3, I3, p253* A cheerful, yellow Triana local with some original and unusual tapas for €1.80 a hit such as aubergine stuffed with prawns. Further down C San Jacinto, cross the road to Bar Oliva, at number 73, and have a piece of swordfish (*pez espada*).

Bodega Siglo XVIII, C Pelay y Correa 32. *1200-2400. Closed Mon. Map 3, I6, p253* A low, quiet bar run by a flamenco artist and decorated in bullfight pictures. The tapas are excellent, modern takes on traditional fare; there's also a big range of *morcillas* from around the nation.

Calle Larga, C Pureza 72. *Tue-Sun 1200-2300. Map 3, I6, p253* Some of the tapas are quite unusual, like *albóndigas de choco* (cuttlefish meatballs), but you're better off going for an old favourite like *riñones al jerez*. The walls are covered with bullfight photos and the Rocío pilgrimage. Staff are old Triana characters.

Casa Diego, Av Santa Cecilia 29, **T** 954 330 609. *0700-0030*. *Map 3, I1, p253* One of a few places on this popular tapas street that specializes in *caracoles* and *cabrillas* (snails). It's what they do well and you can eat them at the bar or out on the terrace; there are few other frills!

El Faro de Triana, Puente Isabel II s/n, **T** 954 336 192. *1200-0100*. *Map 3, G5, p253* This curious yellow building on the Triana end of the bridge has everything a weary traveller could ask for; wonderful river views, cheap and huge tapas portions and massive glasses of beer or wine. The *gambas* are particularly good, as are the *habas con jamón*. The terrace upstairs is one of the top spots in the city; you'll usually have to queue for a table. Recommended.

Jabbazaír Abacería, Ronda de Triana 39, **T** 954 334 414. *1200-2400*. *Map 3, J1, p253* A beautifully decorated deli-bar with tables perched on terracotta pots filled with chickpeas. It's quiet and friendly, frequently with Middle-Eastern music playing. The food is superb; the best of hams, artichokes, asparagus; try the *cogollos con anchoa*.

Cafés

Café Anibal, C Castilla 98, T 954 343 758. *Tue-Sun 1700-0300*. *Map 3, E3, p252* This likeably strange place is more like a house than a café with a variety of rooms and a bar wedged into the stairwell. There's a relaxed, leftish vibe about the place, which is beautifully tiled with a wrought-iron entrance.

Tetería Chef Chaouen, C Pelay Correa 83. *Tue-Sun 1700-2400*. *Map 3, J7, p253* A popular Moroccan-style tea house with low tables, cushions, and *chichas* to smoke fruit tobacco through. One of a few in Triana; the Baghdad Café at Calle Pureza 22, and the Salam at C Luca de Tena 6 are also good and less touristed.

Centro and San Vicente

Restaurants

€€€ **Taberna del Alabardero**, C Zaragoza 20, **T** 954 502 721. *0800-2400. Map 2, D1, p250* This hospitality school is also one of the city's best restaurants. It's pricey but worth it; the menu changes seasonally, but look out for house specials such as *corvina* (sea bass) with spinach, kidneys, and grapes, or succulent beef fillet with blue *cabrales* cheese. There's a good-value set *menú* for €47; for cheaper eats or a coffee, stay downstairs and head to the back.

€ **Casa Salva**, C Pedro del Toro 12, **T** 954 214 115. *Mon-Fri* *1300-1700. Map 3, B7, p252* A colourful and welcoming little lunchtime restaurant with tasty Mediterranean dishes at low prices just near the Museo de Bellas Artes. Recommended.

€ **Jalea Real**, C Santa (Sor) Angela de la Cruz 37, **T** 954 216 103. *Map 4, K5, p255* A sociable little vegetarian café doing some great feel-good food, especially during the day, when there's a *menú* for €6. Friendly and down-to-earth.

€ **Mesón Serranito**, C Alfonso XII 9, **T** 954 218 299, also at C Antonia Díaz and Ronda de Triana. *0900-0100, Sat-Sun 1300-0100. Map 3, A8, p252* A trio of bar-restaurants with hearty, uncomplicated fare, decorated with bulls heads and serving their tails. Quick service, big portions and cheap.

€ **Orsini**, C Reyes Católicos 25B, **T** 954 216 165. *1200-0100. Map 3, G5, p253* A colourful and high-quality pizza joint, which also offers many other menu choices. The pizzas themselves are excellent with a real Italian taste and good size for around €6.

Tapas bars

Bar Europa, C Siete Revueltas 35, **T** 954 221 354. *0800-2400.* *Map 2, B4, p250* A very good tapas bar that's been in business since 1925. It's a long, traditional-looking place with some fairly original food, such as moussaka and partridge paté. The tortilla here is also good.

Bodega Extremeña, C San Esteban 17, **T** 954 417 060. *1200-2400.* *Map 2, B8, p250* A top tapas bar with cheery staff. *Extremeña* means "from Extremadura" and the food and wine are from that region. There are several cheese and cold meat options, as well as some excellent chargrilled pieces of steak and traditional dishes. Try the *migas*, a traditional peasant dish of breadcrumbs, suet, garlic, and ham all mixed together – it tastes a lot better than it might sound.

Bodegón Don Julián, C San Eloy 47, **T** 954 221 625. *0800-1600, 2000-2300. Variable rest day between Mon-Wed.* *Map 3, B8, p252* A big popular place for tapas or a more substantial meal, with hanging hams and a tiled façade. The food is excellent; the *solomillo al whisky* is superb, the lamb is nice, and there's a daily *guiso* which is good value. The adventurous could try *carillada*, pig's cheeks; on a less agressively carnivorous note, there are good breakfasts served with wholemeal breads.

Bodegón El Cangrejo, C San Felipe 13. *Tue-Sun 1200-2400.* *Map 4, L6, p255* This little street buzzes at weekends as crowds mingle from adjacent bars – it's dubbed "el callejón de los locos" (nutters' lane) but it's not that rowdy. This simple bar is great with friendly staff and delicious meaty tapas and *montaditos*; the *pinchito de lomo* kebab is a great snack.

El Rinconcillo, C Gerona 40, **T** 954 223 183. *1300-0100.* *Map 4, K6, p255* An incredibly old bar that was founded in 1670 when the

139

Eating and drinking

large-jawed Habsburgs still ruled Spain. It's an attractive place that's definitely worth a visit. The tapas are good and served till fairly late; the *croquetas* are particularly memorable.

Entre Cárceles, C Faisanes 1, T 679 374 413. *Mon-Fri 2030-0100, Sat 1230-1730, 2030-0200, Sun 1230-1730. Map 2, C3, p250* This tiny bar is prettily tiled and has old wooden beams and shelves, the latter at alarming angles after years of supporting the favourite tipples of a smartish Sevillian set. The tapas and *raciones* are pricey but delicious; try the *gambas* or spicy *huevos a la flamenca*. Some of the finest of sherries are available by the glass, but pride of place goes to a very old and valuable photo of the Virgen de la Macarena.

La Antigua Bodeguita, Plaza del Salvador 6, T 954 561 833. *Map 2, B3, p250* As long as the weather holds, the interior of this popular bar is really just a place to order, as the crowd from here and the bar next door spills out onto the square. It's a great Sevillian scene in its own right, but the tapas are also worthy. Check out *mojama*, cured tuna meat that will either delight or disgust.

Cafés

Caffé Diletto, C San Pablo 41, T 954 212 394. *0800-2330. Map 3, C8, p252* A pleasant café with wooden beams, old brick walls, and a small terrace. There's a good range of teas, coffees and chocolates, backed up by decent Italian icecream, pastries and a few savoury options.

La Campana, C Sierpes 1, T 954 223 570. *0800-2200. Map 4, L2, p255* An institution, the sweet-toothed will love this place for its icecreams and pastries. During Semana Santa, when it's *the* place to have a seat booked, it has an impressive display of pointy caramel *nazarenos*. At other times, try the *yemas* or the *lenguas de almendra*.

Qué Punt, C Carlos Cañal 5. *0830-2400. Map 3, D8, p252*
A comfortable, cool bar with nice wooden furniture and table
lamps. Good for early evening coffee or breakfasts. On a bit of a
German tip, the snacks on offer include pretzels and *weisswurst*.

La Macarena

Restaurants

€€ **Casa Manolo León**, C Guadalquivir 12, **T** 954 373 735. *1330-
1730, 2030-0100. Map 4, F1, p254* Tasty, home-style food with an
emphasis on fresh produce. It's set in an old Sevillian house and has
a pleasant light patio. There's a good-value *menú del día* for €7.20.

€ **El Caserón**, C Javier Lasso de la Vega 9, **T** 954 215 610. *Map 4,
K2, p255* Very atmospheric place with wooden floors, old lanterns
and candles. It's more a place for sitting down and having *raciones*,
which offer better value here. The ham is good, the *secreto* with
cumin sauce excellent, as are the squid brochettes, but its desserts
such as *plátano flambeado* or *dátiles con miel* that win the day.

€ **El Jueves**, C Feria 109, **T** 954 903 369. *Map 4, E4, p255*
A local pizza and tapas joint with plenty of space, tiles, and
intricately worked light fittings. The staff are friendly, the
pizzas good and the atmosphere relaxed.

€ **La Ilustre Víctima**, C Correduría 35 (sometimes called Dr Leta-
mendi), **T** 954 389 490. *1600-0200. Map 4, E4, p255* A popular bar
and eatery that does its own thing and well. With dishes from North
African, Mexican, Andalucían and Greek cuisine, it's an excellent
place to eat and very cheap. The food is served in attractive
terracotta dishes and there are plenty of vegetarian options.
Slow service aside, it's a cool, but friendly place. Recommended.

Tapas bars

El Ambigú, C Feria 47, **T** 954 381 015. *Mon-Sat 0800-0030.*
Map 4, H4, p255 This simple, tiled bar is known for the high quality
of its home-cooked tapas. The specials vary daily – try the *bacalao
macerado*, or munch on some marinated capers on their stalks. The
portions are generous and there's a good *menú del día* for €6.60.

Yebra, C Medalla Milagrosa 3, **T** 954 351 0070. *Tue-Sun 1200-1700,
2000-2400. Map 1, D7, p248* One of Seville's best tapas joints; a
smart, but relaxed place, offering up authentic gourmet food in
tapas portions for around €1.80. It's not often that you'll see
partridge or pheasant on tapas menus, you will here. The only
drawback is that it's so popular getting an order in can be a
nightmare so try and head there early.

Cafés

Bar Plata, C Resolana 2, **T** 954 371 030. *0600-0100. Map 4,
C5, p254* Sumptuously decked out in tiles and wood, this café
is opposite the basilica in Macarena. There's a lovely tiled wall
showing the old barrio and, of course, the Virgin of Macarena
herself in one corner. As well as coffee, there are tapas and
many excellent rich desserts.

Isla de la Cartuja

Cafés

Esfera, C Marie Curie s/n. *Mon-Sat 1030-2400. Map 1, C2, p248*
A pleasant bar-café in the old Expo site, especially in summer,
when you can sit on its terrace and watch the fountains with a
cold beer in hand.

Indulgence
Coffee and pastries are a daily ritual for many sevillanos.

New Town Boulevards

Restaurants

€€ **La Dorada**, Av Ramón y Cajal s/n, Viapol, **T** 954 921 066. *1300-1600, 2000-2400. Map 1, J8, p249* A smart, seafood restaurant, the food is extremely well-prepared and the *pescado frito* is a cut above what you get in most places. The fresh shellfish are another highlight as is the good service. The decor has a nautical air and the clientèle is fairly wealthy.

Tapas bars

La Dona, C Balbino Marrón s/n, **T** 954 631 705. *Map 1, J8, p249* A stylish little tapas option, decorated with photos and pictures of the horse at work and play. The best option is the *montaditos*.

▶ Tapas

One of Seville's many unforgettable images is the tapas waiter, fresh from taking half a dozen orders. Pouring the drinks rapidly, they then bellow the order through the din to the kitchen. By some miracle they hear, and out comes your dish, accompanied by the curious little breadsticks known as *picos*.

Tapas were invented here; some say they originated as a slice of bread placed over a drink to stop flies dropping by for a drink. Whatever the truth, it's here that they do tapas best.

When you get to a bar, the tapas may be clearly displayed, or you may have to ask. A tapa is a snack-sized portion costing €1-2; these often can't be ordered at tables. Half (*media*) and whole *raciones* are meal-sized portions also designed to be shared. *Montaditos* are delicious little toasted sandwiches.

To do tapas the Seville way don't order more than a couple at each place, share each others' dishes, and stay put at the bar, where your bill will often still be totted up in chalk. Locals know what the specialities of each bar are; it's worth asking, and if there's a daily special, order that.

La Huerta de la Buhaira, Av de la Buhaira s/n, **T** 954 990 717. *1100-2230. Map 1, I7, p249* A beautiful retreat; a terrace shaded by vines and palms in a pretty neo-Moorish park. The food's great too and the tapas portions are large. Try a grilled tuna or a salad. Recommended.

Nueva Enramadilla, C José Recuerda Rubio s/n, **T** 954 656 678. *0800-1600, 2000-2300. Variable rest day between Mon-Wed. Map 1, J8, p249* A big, bright and tasty option at the back of the Viapol, this is a place to come for beer and filling tapas before a night out. Worthwhile choices include the *guiso* or *revuelto* special.

Carmona

Restaurants

€€ **Molino de la Romera**, Puerta de Márchena s/n, **T** 954 190 084. Halfway between San Pedro Church and the Alcázar, this restaurant is set in an old olive mill and serves good local cuisine on its terrace, which give views over the plains below.

Ecija

Restaurants

€€ **Las Ninfas**, C Cánovas del Castillo 4, **T** 955 904 592. A stylish restaurant decorated with various *objets d'art* offers well-prepared local cuisine, including some excellent steaks.

Jerez de la Frontera

Restaurants

€€€ **La Mesa Redonda**, C Manuel de la Quintana 3, **T** 956 340 069. *Mon-Sat 1230-1600, 2100-2330.* An established and traditional Jerez restaurant which has gained a well-deserved reputation for itself. Try the several tasty meat dishes in some sort of sherry sauce and a *caldereta* if it's available; these stews are seriously delicious.

Tapas bars

Reino de León, C Latorre s/n, **T** 954 322 915. This unremarkable-looking tapas bar does absolutely superb food. Order whatever the daily special is; if it's *mollejas* (sweetbreads) and you're a fan of innards, it's your lucky day, but everything's really tasty.

Córdoba

Restaurants

€€ **El Churrasco**, C Romero 16, **T** 957 290 819. *1300-1600, 2030-2400. Closed Aug.* Map 5, C4, p256 One of Córdoba's finest restaurants specializing in grilled meats. Set in the heart of the *Judería*, it's advisable to book, as there aren't a lot of tables. The *churrasco* is indeed excellent, offset by a tangy sauce, and there's plenty of attention paid to the service and the wine list.

€€ **Taberna Plateros**, C San Franciso 6, **T** 957 470 042. *Map 5, B8, p256* Opposite Hotel Maestre, this 17th-century bar and restaurant has a large patio decorated with colourful tiles and several small rooms, including one dedicated to the local bullfighter Manolete. The food is solid homestyle cooking with the starters a meal in themselves.

Seville's nightlife can't compete in terms of variety with Barcelona or Madrid, but you certainly won't be left sipping a vodka in an empty bar or dancing salsa with your own shadow.

Seville folk tend to call it a night fairly early midweek and party until sun up come the weekend, but there are plenty of zones which are always fairly lively; particularly around Plaza Alfalfa and Calle Betis in Triana; both populated by a lively mixture of locals and tourists. At weekends things liven up; the Viapol zone has a much more local scene (see box p158), and the Alameda de Hércules buzzes with a fairly alternative scene. There are few *discotecas* that are at the cutting edge of international music, but you can be assured of a cheerful late night out in any of the spots below.

Check the Gay and Lesbian section for a listing of bars *de ambiente* and the Arts and Entertainment section to catch some flamenco, whether it be a scheduled show or a sudden outburst of *duende*.

The cathedral and around

Bars

Antigüedades, C Argote de Molina 40. *2000-0300, Sat-Sun 2000-0400*. *Map 2, D4, p250* A highly unusual bar with a terrace near the cathedral, filled to the rafters with stuffed humanoids in strange poses, a labour of love of the artistic owner. They're accompanied by severed limbs in cages and a buzzy mix of locals, tourists, and reasonably priced drinks.

Pecata Mundi, C Alvarez Quintero 46. *Mon-Wed 2100-0200. Open later Thu-Sun*. *Map 2, D3, p250* A decent bar decorated with paintings of the seven deadly sins; pass the time trying to work out which is which. There's usually an interesting crowd in; and spirit prices are good; try *Flor de Caña*, a tasty Nicaraguan rum. It also does reasonable tapas.

Zapata, C Rodríguez Zapata 1. *Thu-Sun 2100-0100*. *Map 2, D3, p250* A cheerful, red, Mexican bar near the cathedral with, for once, not a fajita in sight – only drinks. Slushy margaritas roll over at one end of the bar and there's plenty of beer and tequila going down too, mostly on the street outside.

Barrio Santa Cruz

Bars

Berlin, C Boteros s/n, **T** 954 221 697. *2000-0700*. *Map 2, A5, p250* Brick-lined bar near Plaza Alfalfa with an interesting and talkative crowd. Run by an Austrian with a perfect Andalucían accent, it's open until all-hours and plays a mix of popular rock. Drinks are relatively cheap, making it a good late night option in this part of town. When you're done, head to Bar Manolo on Plaza Alfalfa and have a *tostada de jamón* with plenty of olive oil – it'll seem like one of the best meals you've ever had.

La Rebotica, C Pérez Galdós 11, **T** 954 221 625. *2100-0300. Map 2, A5, p250* One of a few popular bars on this street, this place is known for its *chupitos*, shooters that'll set you back €1.05 and probably make or break your night out. There are 75 or so to choose from.

South of the cathedral

Clubs

Apandau, Av María Luisa s/n. *2100-0500. Map 2, K5, p251* An attractive, spacious *discoteca* picturesquely set in one of the 1929 exhibition buildings by the Teatro Lope de Vega. Music is mostly Spanish, with plenty of salsa and *merengue* – there are often classes from 2100-2330 before the place fills up.

El Arenal

Bars

Kiosko del Agua, Paseo de Colón s/n. *Apr-Oct 1100-2200. Map 2, H1, p251* On the riverfront, this is one of Seville's best spots for an evening beer. Sit on the wrought-iron metal chairs and watch the sun set over Triana while bats and swallows flutter among the silhouetted palm trees. Good views of the floodlit Torre del Oro too.

★ Grungy bars

Best

- Berlin, p149
- Burbujas, p151
- Taberna Baños, p156
- Antigüedades, p149
- Habanilla Café, p156

Clubs

Party Ship, Paseo Marqués del Contadero s/n. *Map 2, I1, p251*
A glass boat on the river near the Torre del Oro that stages a variety
of club nights in spring and summer. Cover charge is €15 (€13
with a drink if you pre-book) and the music ranges from drum 'n'
bass to house and is sometimes of decent standard. Atmosphere
is capital H happy and locals stash plastic bottles of booze in the
bushes to avoid the costly drinks inside.

Triana

Bars

Burbujas, Corona Center, Pl de la Virgen Milagrosa. *Thu-Sun
2000-0200. Map 3, K7, p253* It's a curiosity of Spanish life that
good bar scenes are often to be found in seedy shopping arcades;
a few bars pool together in this one, where there's a lively crowd
sitting out at plastic tables. It's an excellent place for a few drinks,
there's a non-sceney gay presence too, and litre pitchers of
cocktails are a mere €7.50.

Café de la Prensa, C Betis 8, **T** 954 333 420. *1500-0300.* *Map 3, G5, p253* Lives up to its name with its walls papered with pages from old newspapers; there's a good, quiet late drinking scene here and a down-to-earth crowd most nights. Drinks are cheapish for this stretch and it's also a relaxing place to sit and hang out during the late afternoon.

La Fundición, C Betis 49-50. *2100-0300, weekend 2100-0500.* *Map 3, J7, p253* A big Triana bar which goes late with a cheerily drunk crowd of locals and foreigners. The beer's cold, there's a pool table (though it's not usable when the bar's full), and the music is soft enough to allow the chat-up lines to flow thick and fast. The decor is of the generic American filling station type.

Clubs

Bailodromo, C Castilla 137, **T** 954 342 204. *Wed-Sun 2300-0600.* *Map 3, D2, p252* This sweaty, slightly seedy venue is one of Seville's best for some authentic salsa and *merengue*, as proven by the significant Latin American contingent that shows everyone else how it's done on the dance floor.

Boss, C Betis 67. *Wed-Sun and doesn't shut until about 1800 on weekends.* *Map 3, K8, p253* This fashionable Seville club on the Triana riverfront has disappeared up its own backside a little in recent years, with more attention paid to the door policy than the DJ line-up. That said, it's free entry and there's sometimes some good house music across its spacious interior, which includes four bars.

Río Latino, C Betis 40. *2000-0300, Fri-Sat 0630.* *Map 3, I7, p253* The most local in character of the Calle Betis *discotecas*, this has a youngish Seville set and top-20 Spanish hits. It's fitted out in fairly attractive fake stone. Free entry and easy door policy.

Centro and San Vicente

Bars

Capote, C Arjona s/n. By Puente Isabel II. *Jun-Sep 1100-0300. Map 3, F5, p252* A summer-only open-air bar that looks like it's on a Caribbean beach with palm fronds and relaxed Cuban music. An excellent option for an afternoon beer or a late drink. Frequent live music.

La Fábrica, Centro Plaza De Armas, **T** 954 908 828, www.lafabrica-cerveceros.com *1200-0100 . Map 3, B5, p252* Despite a chain pub feel (it's actually not one), this place near the bus station is worth a visit. They brew their own good beer and there's plenty of sunshine on the terrace. There are also good tapas available.

Nu Yor Café, C Marqués de Paradas 30, **T** 954 212 889. *2300-0400. Map 3, D6, p252* A posh and attractive bar with an air of smart elegance. Set in a high, closed patio and decked out with architectural drawings, there's live jazz and Cuban music here on Thursday-Saturday from 2400. Drinks are fairly pricey and rise later in the night, but there's a decent spirit selection.

Quita Pesares, Pl Jerónimo de Córdoba, **T** 954 229 385. *1200-1600, 2000-0200. Map 4, L7, p255* This cheery bar is run by larger-than-life character, flamenco singer Pepe Peregil. He's a shoo-in for any Spaniard-of-the-month contest and breaks into song at regular intervals between healthy draughts of the excellent barrelled *manzanilla* and slices of *jamón serrano*.

Taboo, C Trastamara 30. *Thu-Sat 2000-0300, Sun 1700-0100. Map 3, C6, p252* A very interesting bar near the bus station with a big range of events from house music nights to flamenco to Sunday afternoon comedy. Attracts a cool, young mixed set but it's not a cliquey place.

Clubs

Bar-Café Seville/Bestiario, C Zaragoza, T 954 213 475. *Mon-Wed 1200-0300, Thu-Sat 1200-0600. Map 2, D1, p250* This café-bar is popular with a suited evening crowd, but as the evening wears on it transforms itself into a *discoteca* with free entry but hefty drink prices. It's open lateish most week nights; despite the name, the crowd is fairly civilized and 30-something, dancing away to Spanish top-20 hits under bluey lights and pseudo-modern decor. Its central location can make this a decent option.

Gaudy Sala, C Julio César 3. *Wed-Sat 2300-0500. €6-10, but look out for promotional flyers that give free entry before 0200. Map 3, C7, p252* A new and upmarket *discoteca*, one of a few options on this street. Decor is modern chrome, and the door policy is relatively strict. Music is generally the latest pop and dance hits, but there are themed Friday funk nights.

La Macarena

Bars

Bar La Sirenas, Alameda de Hércules 34. *1600-0200 (weekends 0400). Map 4, F3, p254* Another lively bar in this zone, much favoured by rockers, punks, and anarchists, who mingle in a cheerful outdoor beer zone.

Bar Santa Marta, Cnr C Daóiz & Angostillo, **T** 954 901 954. *1200-0100. Map 4, K3, p255* A good place for outdoor drinking of an evening with a big terrace in a pretty cobbled square by a church. The tapas and *raciones* are fairly standard but tasty Sevillian fare.

Bulebar Café, Alda de Hércules 82, **T** 954 901 954. *1300-0100. Map 4, G3, p255* One of several good choices on this long promenade, the Bulebar has a nice little terrace and is decorated with rows of coloured disks. It's a popular meeting point for an alternative set and has a relaxed feel about it.

Café del Mar, C Jesús del Gran Poder 83. *1600-0200 (Fri-Sat 0400). Map 4, G2, p255* A cool and stylish set hang out here which is a coffee stop by day and chill-out zone by night. Relaxed but elegant furnishings and likeable staff. Attracts a mixed crowd.

Café Hércules, C Peris Mencheta 15. *1200-2400 (weekends 0200). Map 4, F4, p254* Small bar which attracts a weekend crowd substantially bigger than it. The chatty alternative set spill onto the pavement downing *cubatas* and munching on small bar snacks until lateish. Friendly vibe.

El Goloso en Llamas, C Conde de Barajas s/n. *1200-1500, 1900-0100. Map 4, H2, p255* A curious mixture of a place but a relaxing spot for a drink away from the *marcha* of the Alameda. The walls are decorated with sci-fi posters, but the comfortable tables have candles and a romantic atmosphere.

El Imperdible, Pl San Antonio de Padua 9, **T** 954 388 219. *Map 4, H1, p255* A good leftish café-bar in La Macarena with plenty of students and frequent, diverse events such as poetry readings, live music or art exhibitions.

El Lokal, C Alvaro de Bazán 6. *Map 4, E1, p254* A committed leftist and anarchist meeting place and bar with frequent politically aware gigs and events. Just off the Alameda de Hércules.

Habanilla Café, Alameda de Hércules 63, **T** 954 902 718.
1200-0300. Map 4, F3, p254 Nice, old double-storeyed building
with a balcony and tiled interior. Drop in for coffee during the day
or take advantage of a decent spirit selection by night. One of
three good bars next to each other.

Naïma Café Jazz, C Trajano 47, **T** 954 382 485. *Map 4,
I2, p255* Just off the Alameda de Hércules, this relaxed
and popular weekend jazz bar opens at 2400 and stays open
until 0500 or later as long as there's plenty of folk around.

Taberna Baños, C Baños 34. *Wed-Sun 2000-0100. Map 4, J1,
p255* A relaxed, not-too-crowded barrio bar where locals gather.
With good reason too; they make cracking *caipirinhas* (order them
with *cachaça* for the real Brazilian taste) and have a very good pool
table, so there can be no "dodgy cue" excuses for poor play.

Clubs

Fun Club, Alameda de Hércules 84. *Tue-Sat 2300-0800.
Map 4, H3, p255* A music venue and *discoteca* with some serious
alternative cred in these parts. There's often live rock, drum 'n'
bass, or good DJs; entry is often free otherwise.

Holiday, C Jesús del Gran Poder 73, **T** 954 379 655. *Thu-Sat
2200-0500, Sun 1800-0100, but don't bother before about 0200.
€10 entry includes a drink. Map 4, H2, p253* Behind the Alameda
de Hércules, this massive venue appears comedy kitsch from the
lobby with chandeliers and porcelain urns. The interior is very
different and spacious with modern dance beats.

Weekend, C Torneo 43, **T** 954 909 178. *Thu-Sat 2230-0700. Entry
on Fri and Sat is €10, including a drink. Map 1, E3, p248* Open very
late and doesn't really get going until 0300 or so. One of Seville's

better central *discotecas*. The sound system is good, and there are often live performances. Music varies but it is generally popular house or Spanish and international pop hits.

La Cartuja

Clubs

Antique Teatro, C Matemáticos Rey Pastor y Castro s/n, **T** 954 462 207. *Thu-Sat 2400-0700, but don't turn up until at least 0300. Cover is €10-15 with a drink. Map 1, C3, p248* Probably the best current option for dance with an excellent sound system and committed DJs in one of the old pavilions from the 1992 Expo.

New Town Boulevards

Bars

Atelier, Edificio Viapol s/n. *1100-0100 (Fri-Sat 0500). Map 1, J7, p249* Popular bar with an easygoing crowd dancing to recent Spanish hits and is staffed by friendly folk. By day it's a café and you can sit back and ponder the "cogs 'n' gods" murals..

Clubs

Occidental, Av San Francisco Javier 22. *Thu-Sat 2000-0500. Map 1, J8, p249* A good-looking, if comparatively small, *discoteca* that usually has a good DJ line-up. House music it is, generally slightly harder on Thursday and Friday. Door policy is fairly relaxed and entry is €6, including a drink, which makes it good value compared with others in the area.

A night out in Viapol

If you're looking for a night out away from tourists and pretty plazas, try this modern commercial zone centred around the building of the same name on Calle Enramadilla. Start your evening off at a few of the excellent tapas bars in the streets behind it; *Nueva Enramadilla*, *Jamón Donal's*, and *La Dona* are all good options. With stomach satisfied, you then have many choices, not least of which is the massive, slightly volatile *botellón* that kicks off about midnight in the car park opposite the Viapol building.

Buy some alcohol and head on over– it's a good way to meet young locals. Otherwise, head off to the selection of student bars a block up on Av Ramón y Cajal – *Nueva Epoca* is the best of these – or to one of the pre-club bars around Viapol itself, such as Atelier or O'Neill's for Guinness fans. Finally, there's a good choice of clubs both here or five minutes up the road and round the corner on Av San Francisco Xavier, where Occidental is a decent little place. A cab to or from the cathedral to Viapol will be €3-5 or the zone's about a 10-15 minute walk from the

Wall Street, Edificio Viapol s/n and **El Palco**. *Thu-Sat 2300-0600. Both cost €10 with drink at peak times. Cheaper entry before 2400.* Map 1, J7, p249 Wall Street is one of the better *discotecas* in the Viapol zone – a fairly upmarket venue with music centering on *latino*. Sometimes there are free salsa classes from 2300. El Palco is another decent option in the same zone.

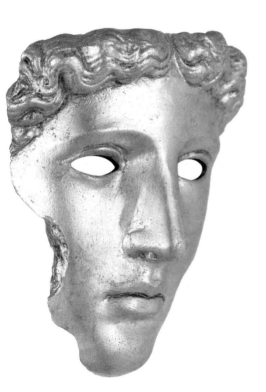

Whether you're planning to spend hours trawling bars in search of the most authentic *cante jondo* or just want to briefly experience what it's all about, it's likely you'll want to see some flamenco while you're in Seville. While much of what's on offer is geared to tourists (although frequently of a very high technical standard), it's still possible to track down a more authentic experience. Although it's far from true to say flamenco is the only cultural form on offer in Seville, it is probably correct to say its popularity has hindered the development of other types of drama, dance, and music in the city.

While Seville has a handful of theatres, it's certainly not the place to come for opera and ballet. That said, what drama exists is generally of a high standard, and many of the cafés and bars around the Alameda de Hércules put on regular, low-key cultural events. Your best guide to upcoming events is *El Giraldillo*, (www.elgiraldillo.es) *Cultura en Seville* is another free publication worth checking as is *The Tourist* (all available at tourist offices). Also try http://sevillahoy.net and www.hispalis.net

Cinema

Most cinema sessions cost €4-5, although it's usually cheaper before evening. All cinemas have a *día del espectador*, usually Wednesday, when admission is €3. Always be prepared for a long ticket queue at popular times, like Sunday evenings.

Alameda Cine, Alameda de Hércules 9, **T** 954 915 762. *Map 4, H3, p255* Convenient cinema just off the Alameda de Hércules; **Avenida V.O**, C Marqués de Paradas 15, **T** 954 293 025. *€4.80, and €3 Mon or any session before 1800. Map 3, A6, p252* A good cinema complex showing mostly original version films subtitled in Spanish. Handy late-opening food hall next door; **Cervantes**, C Amor de Dios s/n, **T** 954 915 681. *Map 4, I3, p255* Another cinema near the Alameda; **Corona**, C Salado, **T** 954 278 064. *Map 3, L7, p253* A small cinema in Triana.

Dance

Flamenco and sevillanas rule the dance roost in Seville and there are few venues dedicated to other forms of movement. That said, the theatres listed below often have dance performances from local or international touring ensembles. See *El Giraldillo* for upcoming performances.

Flamenco

There are essentially three ways to see flamenco in Seville. The *tablaos* are organized performances in set venues with entry ranging from €10-25. The crowd at these is mostly tourists, the performers often well-known and of a very high standard, and the emotion factor usually very low. Secondly, there are many bars that have dedicated flamenco nights; the quality varies according to the artist and the atmosphere, the cost is minimal, and occasionally you'll see something very special. Thirdly, in bars where flamenco enthusiasts hang out, you may well see some impromptu performances. Look for likely local bars in Triana and La Macarena and hang around keeping a lowish profile.

Abacería Rebeca, C Arfe 11. *Opens fairly late, even during the week.* *Map 2, F2, p250* A very pleasant, old bar with deli products that does simple tapas like ham and paté as well as hot dogs on occasion. There are live performances on Friday and Saturday nights, usually flamenco, and you might be lucky enough to catch some impromptu stuff at other times. It's a cosy place with pretty shelves and an upstairs area with hand painted tables and chairs.

Associación Antigua Sevilla, C Castelar 50, **T** 954 210 512. *Map 3, E8, p253* A small, cultural organization that fairly regularly puts on good, cheap flamenco performances as well as other music and dance events.

Bar Anselma, C Pagés del Corro 49. *Map 3, H3, p253* A busy and beautifully decorated Triana bar with free entry but expensive drinks. There's live music every night but Sunday; it tends to be popular Seville ditties rather than pure flamenco, but it can be entertaining, particularly when Anselma herself is in form.

Casa de la Memoria de Al-Andalus, C Ximénez de Enciso 28, **T/F** 954 560 670. *Map 2, E6, p250* See Music below.

El Mundo, C Siete Revueltas 5, **T** 954 215 335. *Map 2, A4, p250* Tucked into the crooked backstreets near Plaza Alfalfa, this tunnel-like bar offers up free flamenco on Tuesday nights. Opening about 2300, it's not really worth going until midnight or so. The show normally starts about 0030; the quality is variable but usually reasonable, and the crowd is a mixture of tourists and locals. Drink prices are slightly beefed up to cover the costs of the performance.

El Palacio Andaluz, Av María Auxiliadora 18, **T** 954 534 720. *Map 1, F7, p248* A touristy restaurant and *tablao* that generally has a fairly high standard of performances. A fixture for years; you can definitely have a good night here, but you'll dine better for less elsewhere.

El Tamboril, Plaza Santa Cruz s/n, **T** 954 561 590. *Map 2, F6, p250* A small, cheerful bar with plenty of tourists as well as locals. There's live music daily from midnight until 0300; it's usually *rociera*; there's a replica of the Virgin of Rocío taking pride of place in the centre of the bar; sevillanas are also popular.

El Tejar, C San Jacinto 68. *Map 3, J2, p253* A bar with a good quiet atmosphere, see-through tables and art on the red walls. There's live flamenco on most Friday evenings.

La Carbonería, C Leviés 18, **T** 954 214 460. *Until 0330. Map 2, D6, p250* Long-established, popular, sprawling bar, a former coal yard where flamenco is performed at 2230 every night. It's very touristy, but there's sometimes a strong gypsy presence too and some of the flamenco is very good. There's also a late-running tapas counter, a beer garden, and a front bar with free jazz or funk. Free (but the drinks are slightly pricier than normal).

La Sonanta, C San Jacinto 31 (also Plaza Chapina 22), **T** 954 343 185. *Map 3, H4, p253* A pair of stalwart Triana bars with frequent live flamenco by good local performers. At the time of writing this was on Tuesday (San Jacinto) and Thursday (Plaza Chapina), but ring to check.

La Zapata, C Betis 39, **T** 954 001 051. *Until 0300-ish at weekends. Map 3, I7, p253* A local Triana bar oblivious to the trendies and tourists in the rest of the street. It's popular with flamenco enthusiasts and you may well see a top impromptu performance if you lurk about for a while.

The tiling's on the wall

The Virgen del Rocío, beautifully created in tiles, whose Whitsun pilgrimage the faithful attend from Seville and across Spain.

Las Columnas de Acaya, C Virgen de Fátima 9. *Map 3, L3, p253*
A local Triana joint, completely untouristy, with some sort of
flamenco most weekends.

Los Gallos, Plaza de Santa Cruz 11, **T** 954 216 981, www.tablaolos
gallos.com *€21 and includes a drink*. *Map 2, F6, p250* This is a
touristy *tablao* but definitely one of the best of its kind, with
high-quality performers who don't all seem to be going through
the motions. There are two shows a night; go to the later one.

Peña Flamenca Alameda, C Lumbreras 12, and **El Bollo**,
C Fabié 5. *Map 4, E2, p254 and Map 3, H5, p253* *Peñas* are social
clubs organized by groups of people with a particular interest.
These are two of many specializing in flamenco; there are often live
performances at weekends. Exercise tact; they are essentially bars
for members and not tourists, but you'll have no problems getting
in providing you respect that fact.

Sol Café Cantante, C Sol 5, **T** 954 225 165. *Map 4, J8, p255*
Young flamenco artists perform live here every Thursday-Saturday
nights from 2100. The quality is usually high and the price
reasonable at €12.

Universidad de Sevilla. *Map 2, L4, p251* There's typically a free
performance every two to four weeks during term-time, usually at
the Pabellón de Uruguay on Av de Chile, where information will be
displayed on the noticeboards.

Music

The main venues for classical concerts are the theatres (see below).
For live music, see also the Bars section and *La Carbonería* and
Associación Antigua Sevilla in the Flamenco section. *El Giraldillo* is
the best guide to upcoming performances.

Casa de la Memoria de Al-Andalus, C Ximénez de Enciso 28, **T/F** 954 560 670, memorias@teleline.es *€11. Box office: Mon-Sun 0900-1400, 1800-2100; visits finish 2000 (€1).* *Map 2, E6, p250* A beautifully decorated house worth a look in its own right for its pretty patio and Moorish ambience. It's also a cultural centre – there's regular, high-quality flamenco, but also other intriguing concerts, often on a Middle Eastern theme. The shows usually start at 2100 or 2230. Be sure to book in advance.

El Cafetal, Av Ciudad Jardín 5. A café-bar with frequent live music of different kinds, predominantly with a world/roots leaning. Quiet atmosphere but quality is often excellent.

Theatre

Seville's three principal theatres all put on a range of drama, music, and dance. The Maestranza is the most mainstream; at both the other venues there's more avant-garde programming and significantly cheaper tickets.

Teatro Central, C José de Gálvez s/n, **T** 954 460 780 *Map 1, C3, p248* On the Isla de la Cartuja, this serves up a good range of mostly contemporary drama and music.

Teatro Lope de Vega, Av María Luisa s/n, **T** 954 590 853. *Map 1, K5, p249* This lovely building built for the 1929 exhibition has some excellent theatre and music at bargain prices; tickets for some events are as cheap as €4.

Teatro de la Maestranza, Paseo Colón 22, **T** 954 226 573, www.teatromaestranza.com *Ticket office, daily 1000-1400, 1800-2100.* *Map 2, G1, p251* This acclaimed modern building is Seville's principal venue for opera, drama, and dance. It's a fairly dressy scene.

Fiestas play a major part in Spanish life and nowhere more than in Seville. The solemn Semana Santa processions during Easter week are unforgettable, while the subsequent Feria de Abril cheerfully combines three Andalucían icons; *flamenca* costumes, horses and copious quantities of sherry. These major events take their toll and the city is comparatively quiet for the rest of the year, although there's usually something on or pending. With Seville's penchant for the picturesque, it's well worth planning your trip to coincide with one of the following events, but bear in mind that for the major ones, you'll be paying substantially more for accommodation and should reserve rooms in advance.

It's by no means possible to list all the enjoyable fiestas held through summer around the province. Every village, no matter how small, has its two or three days of non-stop partying and going to one is an unforgettable Spanish experience. Ask at the tourist office for any that might coincide with your visit.

January

Cavalcada de los Reyes Magos (5 January) There is an exuberant parade of the Three Kings through the streets. They travel in colourful horse carriages and toss sweets and gifts to onlookers.

February

Carnaval/Shrove Tuesday A big event in Carmona and Córdoba (and especially Cádiz), less so in Seville. Dressing up is definitely advised. The main day is Shrove Tuesday, 47 days before Easter Sunday and the weekend before it.

March/April

Semana Santa (Easter week is 4-11 April 2004, 20-27 March 2005, 9-16 April 2006 and 1-8 April 2007) The most famous of Spain's Easter weeks is in Seville. Members of the city's 52 *cofradías* parade *pasos* of Christ and the Virgin through the city streets. The floats are accompanied by hooded *nazarenos* and cross-carrying *penitentes*. See box on the next page. Córdoba's processions are also worthwhile.

April

Feria de Abril (Feria is 27 April-2 May 2004, 12-17 April 2005, 25-30 April 2006, 24-29 April 2007.) Feria originated as a livestock market but has now become the major social event of the Seville calendar. Upwards of a thousand *casetas* (small pavilions) see a week of eating and drinking *manzanilla*, while during the day the townsfolk parade their pretty horse carriages and *flamenca* dresses. See box p66. (The venue is due to change in a few years.)

Semana Santa

Seville's Holy Week processions are an unforgettable sight. Mesmeric candlelit lines of hooded figures and cross-carrying penitents make their way through the city streets accompanied by the mournful notes of a brass band and two large *pasos*, one with a scene from the Passion, one with a statue of Mary. These scenes aren't unique in Spain but what makes it so special is the Sevillians' extraordinary respect and interest for the event and devotion to the sculptures.

But while other nations eat chocolate eggs and hot cross buns, why are things so serious here? In Seville, at least, the Semana Santa processions as we know them today evolved at a time when things were going wrong. As the Spanish crown lurched into financial meltdown in the 17th century, Seville, the economic hub of the country, went with it. The population declined as merchants left to seek better markets and the plague of the middle of the century killed an astonishing 50% of those who were left, testament to the squalid living conditions of the once-prosperous city. It seemed that God was punishing Seville, and penance and atonement became the order of the day. Today, members of nearly 60 *cofradías* (brotherhoods) practise intensively for their big moment, when they leave their home church or chapel and walk through the streets to the *carrera oficial*, a route leading along Calle Sierpes to the cathedral (and a much-needed toilet break) and then home again. Some of the brother-hoods have well over a thousand in the parade; these consist of *nazarenos*, who wear pointed hoods (adopted by the KKK, but designed to hide the face of a man repentant before God), *penitentes*, who carry crosses (many of the *nazarenos* and *penitentes* go barefoot), and *costaleros*, who carry the *pasos*. It's a keenly-sought honour but it's seriously hard work, sweating away under velvet curtains while carrying upwards of 50 kilos apiece on their shoulders; several of those brotherhoods that live furthest away are on the street for more than 12 hours. The *costaleros* are directed by a *capataz*, who tells them when to start and stop, and encourages them onwards. Each *paso* is accompanied by a band who play processional music, haunting brass laments accompanied by deep thuds of drums.

The *pasos* themselves are canopied floats aglitter with embroidery and candles. The sculptures vary from recent creations to 17th century masterpieces but share some traits; the Christs are anguished, baroque figures and the Virgin Marys are sad, but beautiful and introspective, dressed in much finery for the occasion.

The first brotherhoods walk on Palm Sunday and the processions continue up until Easter Sunday, when a single *cofradía* celebrates the Resurrection. The most important series of processions are on the night of Maundy Thursday (*la madrugá*), when several of the most important brotherhoods make their way to the cathedral during the wee hours.

Sevillians hold the processions in great esteem, and a high percentage are members of a *cofradía*, even if they're not really religious. Everyone has their favourite sculpture too; the best-loved Virgins are La Macarena and La Triana, and you'll visit few bars without a picture of one or the other. The most admired Christs are *El Cachorro* and *Jesús del Gran Poder*, both supreme pieces of art. During the processions, it's not uncommon for people on the street or on balconies to launch into a *saeta*, a haunting flamenco-based song inspired by the *paso*; similarly, the Virginss are often greeted with shouts of "guapa!" by people entranced by their beauty.

▶ Semana Santa Essentials

Supplies: Pick up a copy of the programme, free in bookshops from the previous week. Buy a map with a street index to track routes. Wear sun cream if it's a hot day, but don't bother with an umbrella; the *cofradías* stay home if it's wet, as the rain would damage the *pasos*. They are not rescheduled, but have to wait until next year.

What to see and where to see them: If you're in Seville for the week, you'll see plenty of processions, so there's no point rushing around trying to see all of them. Pick a couple during the early part of the week, and go hard on the Thursday night.

The streets are crowded, but you'll still get a good view from most parts of the route. The most crowded places are around the church and in the streets near the cathedral (although the *carrera oficial*, the last stretch into the cathedral, is seating-only). There are generally a lot less people on the *cofradía's* return journey. Serious photographers will want to

stake out a spot early. The seating along the *carrera oficial* is mostly occupied by long-time local subscribers, but there are some seats available, which you can nab by going in the early morning and paying the attendants who look after each block. The price will vary according to the day and location, but is usually €25-40. The view is great, but it can be boring sitting in one place; much of the excitement is in seeking them out or coming across them by chance.

Some of the most interesting are: **La Paz (Palm Sunday)**. A spectacular sight coming up C San Fernando, best seen from the fountain in Puerta de Jerez, where it passes around 1500. **San Esteban** (Tuesday). Their exit (1500) and entry (2230-2330) from a church just behind the Casa de Pilatos is great to watch as the manoeuvring of the *pasos* is a difficult feat. Get there a long time before though. **Las Siete Palabras** (Wednesday). This 16th-century *cofradía* has an excellent Calvary as one of their three *pasos*. See them best from the square in front of the Museo de Bellas Artes from about 2030. **La Madrugá**: Late on Thursday night, six of the most important *cofradías* make the journey. It's worth making the effort to stay up all night, as most of the city does. First up is **El Silencio**: This 14th-century brotherhood is one of the oldest. Although it's not completely silent, it's black-robed *nazarenos* are an eerie sight. See it from Plaza del Duque from 0100 and stay there for Jesús del Gran Poder. As soon as you've seen the Christ, go north to the Alameda de Hércules, where the procession of La Macarena should be on the way. The Virgin herself will be greeted with rapture here in her own heartland. At about 0430 try and be at the Puente de Triana to watch her great rival La Esperanza de Triana cross the river. If you're still on two feet, make your way up to Plaza Encarnación to see Los Gitanos,

the well-loved gypsy *cofradía*. **El Cachorro/La O** (Friday). If you didn't see La Triana crossing the river, you've got another chance. These two popular Triana *cofradías* simultaneously cross the Puente de San Telmo and the Puente de Triana on their way home at 2330 or so. **La Resurrección** (Sunday). Leaving their Macarena home at 0400-0500, they reach the cathedral about 0800, where there's enough room, and are the last of the processions.

Etiquette: Be silent when watching the *pasos*, and don't applaud unless other people are. Many people consider it rude to cross a procession; definitely don't do it in front of the *paso* or among the band.

What to eat: Crucial is *torrijas*, slices of bread soaked in milk and honey and fried, and *pestiños*, little fried nuggets of honey and dough with a Moorish feel. You'll also see people munching on the offcuts of communion hosts, sold at convents.

Religious conversion
The Giralda, the minaret-turned-cathedral tower,
Seville's iconic symbol.

May

Feria de Jerez It's Jerez's turn for a feria in early May. It's similar, but there's a more serious horsey aspect and the motorcycle Grand Prix tends to be scheduled at the same time.

May/June

Romería del Rocío A picturesque, moving and seriously boisterous pilgrimage to the sanctuary of the Virgen del Rocío in Huelva province. Leaving from all over Andalucía, people descend on the small town in all manner of transport, including colourful ox carts. The Seville contingent leaves from Triana, usually on the Wednesday before Pentecost (the Monday itself, 50 days after Easter Sunday, is the big day at the sanctuary).

Corpus Christi (The Thursday 60 days after Easter Sunday) There are important processions in Seville featuring a variety of well-loved religious images.

Fiestas de Nuestra Señora de la Salud Córdoba's major fiesta is a big week at the end of May. Set by the Guadalquivir, there are horse parades and plenty of dancing and drinking in *casetas*.

July

Potaje de Utrera A major and authentic flamenco festival in the town of Utrera, easily reached from Seville on the local train.

International Guitar Festival In Córdoba starting on the first Sunday of the month. Mostly classical and flamenco forms.

Velá de Santa Ana Triana's patron has her fiesta from the 24-26 July with solemn processions and much dancing and drinking.

Bienal de Flamenco Held every September in even years, this major flamenco event is held in various venues around the city. For further information check www.andalucia.com/flamenco/bienal.htm and www.flamenco-world.com

---

Fiesta de la Inmaculada (Night of the 7 December) *Tunas* (traditional, student minstrel bands) gather in the Plaza del Triunfo by the cathedral and sing traditional songs. In the morning the traditional *Danza de los Seises* is performed by children in the cathedral.

Shopping

Seville's main shopping zone is in Centro around Calles Sierpes, Tetuán, Velásquez, Cuna and Plaza del Duque. This busy area is the place to come for clothes, be it modern Spanish gear or essential Seville Feria fashion; shawls, *flamenca* dresses, *mantillas*, ornamental combs, castanets and fans.

Head to the Alameda de Hércules area for more offbeat shopping, either in the area's lively markets or the smaller shops along Calles Amor de Díos, Jesús del Gran Poder or Trajano. If it's gorgeous ceramics you're after, Triana is the place to go; there are dozens of attractively decorated shops. Most of these shops are used to tourists and can arrange reasonably priced secure international delivery. If you're not an EU resident, remember to pick up an IVA-exemption form; you can get this sales tax refunded at the airport when you leave.

Shops are generally open Monday-Friday 1000-1400, 1700-2030 and Saturday 1000-1400. During Semana Santa, virtually nothing opens on the Thursday, Friday, or Sunday, and many shops are shut the whole week.

Books

Antonio Castro, Pasaje de Andreu 4, **T** 954 217 030. *Map 2, F5, p251* Nice, old second-hand bookshop in the Barrio Santa Cruz with a respectable selection of English paperbacks.

Interbook, Av Luís Montoto 65. *Map 1, H8, p249* An interesting "electronic" bookshop with email access and internet searches as well as plenty of paper titles.

La Casa del Libro, C Velásquez 8, **T** 954 502 950. *Map 2, A2, p250* Good, large bookshop for any needs including travel or English language.

The English Book Shop, Av Eduardo Dato 36. Plenty of English titles.

Ceramics

Cerámica Aracena, C Sierpes. *Map 2, B2, p250* A good place to buy Sevillian tiles and other painted ceramics. Some of the tiles are hand painted in the shop itself which can be interesting to watch.

Cerámica Santa Ana, C Callao 12. *Map 3, G4, p253* One of several excellent ceramics shops in this part of Triana, the traditional home of the industry.

Martian, C Sierpes 74. *Map 2, B3, p250* A pricey ceramics shop near the Plaza San Francisco that sells some very attractive tiles and pots and can arrange worldwide delivery.

Shopping

Department stores

El Corte Inglés, Pl del Duque 7 & 13, **T** 954 220 931. *Map 4, L1, p255* Av Luís Montoto 122, **T** 954 571 440. *Map 1, H8, p249* Pl Magdalena 1, **T** 954 218 855. *Map 2, B1, p250* C San Pablo 1, **T** 954 218 855. *Map 2, B1, p250* Spain's premier department store.

Fashions

Abanicos de Sevilla, Pl San Francisco 7. *Map 2, C3, p250* All types and qualities of fans as well as some fancy shawls.

Adolfo Dominguez, C Sierpes 12. *Map 4, L2, p255* Smart men's (and some women's) fashion from a famous Spanish rag-trade man. Both business and casual wear, medium-priced.

Bershka, Pl de Armas shopping centre and several other stores. *Map 3, B5, p252* A cheap and cheerful Spanish fashion store for girls that are young or young at heart.

Casa Rubio, C Sierpes 56. *Map 2, B2, p250* Fans of all qualities and prices, some remarkable hand painted ones. There are also some attractive *peinas* (hair combs) that are a crucial part of Feria fashion.

Cortefiel, C Tetuan 22. *Map 2, B2, p250* Classic elegant, fashion for ladies of all ages, but with more to offer in the 30-plus ranges.

Diza, C Tetuan 7. *Map 2, B2, p250* Some very pricey but well-made *chales, montones, and mantillas* (shawls, wraps and head-shawls). There are also some *abanicas* (lovely fans); top examples cost more than paying a couple of servants to follow you round all year cooling you down with palm leaves and ostrich feathers.

Flamenkeo, C Recaredo 12, **T** 647 004 577. *Map 2, B2, p250*
An expensive flamenco outfit hire place.

Juan Foranda, C Tetuan 28. *Map 2, B2, p250* A stylish shop
selling the latest Feria fashion including colourful flamenco
dresses, *mantillas* and Córdoban silver jewellery.

Mango, C Velázquez 7. *Map 2, A2, p250* Also in Plaza de Armas
shopping centre. Massive but cool Barcelona-based chain peddling
fashion to trendy, young ladies.

María Rosa, C Cuna 13. *Map 2, A3, p250* Good for flamenco
dresses and Feria fashion for men and women; also a selection
of the colourful Sevillian earrings to go with the dresses.

Sevilla Mágica, Pl de Armas shopping centre. *Map 3, B5, p252*
A place to buy shawls, wraps, fans and other Andalucían essentials.
Some expensive handmade items, but also some decent cheaper
options.

Stradivarius, C Tetuan 2. *Map 2, B2, p250* Fashion *provocativo*
for women of 15-30 or those who like to flaunt it a little.

Sub Urban, C Trajano 44. *Map 4, I2, p255* A shop for streetwear
in hip-hop and similar styles near the Alameda de Hércules.

Torero, Pl de Armas shopping centre. *Map 3, B5, p252* Fairly
smart but low-priced fashion for youngish women.

Velásquez Once, C Velásquez 11. *Map 2, A2, p250* Some good
Sevillian women's fashion. Also a good selection in larger sizes
unlike some of the stores in these parts.

Victorio & Lucchino, C Sierpes 87. *Map 2, B3, p250* José Luís Medina del Corral and José Victor Rodríguez Caro, the former Sevillian, the latter Cordoban, are Spain's best known catwalk designers, and their *prêt-a-porter* creations are very wearable, bright with the light and colours of Andalucía.

Zabol, C Sierpes 16. *Map 2, A2, p250* One of several places to buy trendy Spanish Camper shoes. The showier pairs have designs that extend across both shoes; they're all well-made and last a long time.

Zara, C Velázquez 1 and elsewhere. *Map 2, A2, p250* With stores all over the city, this nationwide chain offers elegant rags in a fairly Spanish style for 18-30 blokes, girls and kids. The label has been successful in Britain and elsewhere; there's more variety to be had here, and also lower prices.

Ziro's, C Tetuan 11. *Map 2, B2, p250* A cool shoe shop with original designs as well as trendy fashion labels.

Food and drink

Baco, C Cuna 4. *Mon-Sat 0930-1430, 1700-2100.* *Map 4, L3, p255* A good deli with several branches around town. Spanish and foreign products, good for classy picnic fare.

La Casa de los Licores, Alameda de Hércules 7 and elsewhere. *Map 4, I3, p255* A very good selection of wines and spirits.

Más, C Arjona 11. *Map 3, C5, p252* A supermarket not far from the Plaza de Armas bus station.

Mercado del Arenal, C Pastor y Landero s/n. *Map 3, E7, p252* A down-at-heel market with a decent large supermarket inside. On the site where Seville's major prison once stood.

Supersol, C Salado s/n. *Map 3, L7, p253* A big Triana supermarket.

Vinotempo, C Don Remondo 3, **T** 954 210 659. *Mon-Fri 1000-1400, 1700-2030, Sat 1100-1430*. *Map 2, E4, p250* A good, smart wine shop with an overseas delivery service and regular tastings.

Markets

Seville has some excellent street markets. A famous flea market takes place on Sunday mornings in the Alameda de Hércules; there is a smaller one on Thursday too. The big Thursday event, *el jueves*, takes place on nearby Calle Feria, when the whole street is filled with stalls of every description. Plaza Alfalfa has a curious Sunday morning animal market.

El Postigo, C Arfe s/n, **T** 954 560 013. *Map 2, F1, p250* This large, indoor craft market is an excellent place to buy ceramics or other handcrafts. There are regular exhibitions and a good range of shops.

Mercado de Abastos, C Castilla s/n. *Map 3, G5, p253* A good undercover food market in Triana that is busiest in the mornings.

Music

Sevilla Rock, C Alfonso XII 1. *Map 4, L1, p255* Wide selection including a big rock section.

Totem Tanz, C Amor de Dios 66, **T** 954 901 994. *Map 4, I3, p255* Specializes in dance music.

Union Records, C Pérez Galdós 4, **T** 954 226 808. *Map 2, A5, p250* Interesting range of music including plenty of *Sevillanas*.

Other

Bordados Carmen, C San Eloy 53. *Map 2, A1, p250* A fairly typical Spanish embroidery shop; a traditional Spanish product that is still significant and very well priced.

Cayuela, C Zaragoza 2. *Map 3, D7, p252* A shop selling a good range of classical guitars with helpful and knowledgeable service.

Celis, Plaza de San Francisco 14. *Map 2, C2, p250* Touristy, but some good T-shirts, posters, and bullfighting paraphernalia on offer.

City Art Gallery, C Aguilas 14. *Map 2, B6, p250* A good little art shop and gallery.

Ciudad de Londres, C Cuna 30. *Map 2, A3, p250* Materials for Sevillian dresses sold out of a beautiful building in the shopping district.

Entre Arte, Paseo de Colón 19. *Map 3, H8, p253* A shop selling dolls and dolls houses in a beautiful building on the riverfront.

Illerina, C Lagar s/n. *Map 2, C2, p250* An interesting shop with a New Age range of materials, curios and accessories.

La Cava de Betis, C Betis 36, **T** 954 278 185. *Map 3, J8, p253* If cigars are your thing, you'll be in heaven here. Excellent selection and service.

Nectar, Pl de Armas shopping centre. *Map 3, B5, p252* A place to buy natural oils, soaps and bodycare products.

Spain's biggest selling daily paper is *Marca*, a publication devoted solely to sport and nearly wholly to football. Its main competitor, *As*, comes in fourth or fifth. This gives some idea of the importance of *fútbol* in Spanish life; a Sunday afternoon generally consists of a massive late lunch, a token stroll, and going with the family down to a local bar to watch the football with a beer and a tapas or two. Watching one of the two big Seville teams play is worth doing, not least for the fact that you'll then have hours of potential conversation with locals at your fingertips.

Bullfighting is also big in Seville, but doesn't have the same cross-sectional appeal. If you're interested in the bulls, La Maestranza is something of a temple and a visit is a must; if you're opposed to it, if you don't like it here, you won't like it anywhere.

Bring your swimming costume even if you don't head down to the coast. At five in the afternoon with the temperature hovering at a humid 38º C the public pool will seem like paradise.

Bullfighting

Bullfighting is the most controversial of activities but very popular in Seville; Andalucía is really the cradle of *los toros*. Seville's bullring, La Maestranza, is the second most prestigious in Spain and draws the top fighters every year. Unless you're sure you'll hate it, consider going just for the Seville fashion and the pure Spanishness of the experience. Seville has around 28 bullfights a season, one every day in Feria, then every Sunday until September. The highest standard can be seen at Feria and at the season's end, but you'll pay more for tickets at these times and they are harder to get hold of. For the big fights, it's worth reserving several days in advance at the ticket office at the bullring, or using one of the agents on Puerta de Jerez or Calle Tetuán, who add on a small commission. Tickets in the sun (*sol*) are the cheapest, followed by *sol y sombra* (sun and shade) and *sombra*. Within the sections, ringside seats (*barreras*) are the most expensive.

Football

While international matches will mostly now be played at the new Estadio Olímpico, the city's two main clubs, Betis and Sevilla, have their own stadiums. Going to a match can be a great experience; there's much more of a family atmosphere than in the majority of European countries. One of the two teams will be at home almost every weekend of the Spanish season. Games are normally on Sunday at 1800, but check the fixtures as there are always Saturday games and a later Sunday kick-off too. You can buy tickets at the grounds during business hours or before the match; they don't sell

!
One Real Betis supporter never misses a home game – even though he died several years ago. His son originally renewed Dad's season ticket and placed the urn with his ashes on the seat at every match; after complaints from the club, he now keeps them on his lap in a cardboard box.

out unless they're playing Real Madrid, Barcelona, or the local derby. Agencies on Calle Tetuán also sell tickets for a small mark-up. Tickets are pricey, with the cheapest seats starting at about €25, depending on the opposition.

Real Betis Balompié, Estadio Manuel Ruíz de Lopera, Av de la Palmera s/n, **T** 954 610 340, www.realbetisbalompie.es Traditionally representing the working class of the city, Betis play in green and white stripes. They are traditionally fairly competitive, but have won the league only once, in 1935. The crowd favourite at the moment is the controversial young forward Dani.

Sevilla FC, Estadio Sanchéz Pizjuan, Av Eduardo Dato s/n, **T** 954 535 353, www.Sevillafc.es The other half of the city's football culture; Seville play in white and red and won the league in 1946. Currently a team of few stars but a solid defence, Seville's best prospect is the young striker José Antonio Reyes.

Skydiving

Skydive Spain, **T** 678 849 554 (English), **T** 687 227 870 , **F** 954 153 287, www.skydivespain.com   A company running static line jumps, tandem dives (€200) and skydiving courses not far from Seville.

Swimming

Piscina Alfarería, C Alfarería 125, **T** 954 340 122. *Map 3, D1, p252* A heated public pool in Triana. Busy at weekends.

Watersports

Pedalquivir *Map 3, H8, p253* Rental of rowboats, pedalos, canoes and more on the riverbank not far from the bullring.

Seville's gay scene isn't a patch on Madrid's or Barcelona's, but as you'd expect from a medium-sized European city, you're not short of options. Seville has a sizeable gay and lesbian population and it's significantly boosted by tourists in season. Community attitudes are perhaps not quite 21st century in general, particularly among the older generations, but gay and lesbian visitors should encounter no problems at all and will feel accepted in nearly all bars and clubs.

The area around the Alameda de Hércules is a good hunting ground for both gay nightlife and gay-friendly nightlife, but there are plenty of options scattered through the city. The venues listed here are those that are predominantly gay and lesbian, but that's not to say there aren't plenty of folk that stay away from the scene; most *discotecas* have at least an element at weekends.

Both Seville's major saunas come highly recommended and the AireSeville guesthouse is as pleasant a place to stay as you could hope for in the centre of the old town.

Guesthouses

AireSeville, C Aire s/n, **T** 954 500 905, **F** 606 599 365,
www.aireseville-gay.com *Map 2, D5, p250* A gay guesthouse
in a quiet street in Barrio Santa Cruz that makes an excellent
place to stay. There's a variety of beautifully decorated a/c
rooms, some with exterior bathroom, and a large, docile dog.
The price ranges from €60-70 per double; this includes breakfast
on a shady terrace and superb hospitality from the owner. A
sunny terrace above gives views of the Giralda: all in all, it's a
top option. Highly recommended.

Bars and clubs

El 27, C Trastamara 27. *2100-0300 (weekends 0700).* *Map 3,
C6, p252* A discreet, backstreet bar attracting mostly gay
males. Relaxing atmosphere and music.

El Hombre y El Oso, C Amor de Dios 32, www.elhombre
yeloso.net *2230-0230, weekends 0330. Door policy is men only.*
Map 4, I3, p255 A large bar with three levels, a *cuarto oscuro*
(darkroom), videos and cubicles. It's virtually wholly gay male;
as the name would suggest, there are plenty of bears, but that's
by no means the whole story.

El Mundo, C Siete Revueltas 5, **T** 954 215 335. *2300-0300.*
Map 2, A4, p250 This bar varies in atmosphere according to what's
on. Apart from Tuesday night flamenco, there's usually a fair gay
and lesbian element, and it's always an interesting spot for a drink.

El Paseo & Isbiliyya, Paseo de Colón 2, **T** 954 210 460.
2000-0300, weekends 0600. *Map 3, E6, p252* Two adjacent gay
bars right opposite the Triana bridge with a nice outdoor terrace.

There's plenty of dancing and music and live shows at weekends. Due to their prime location and cheerful atmosphere they attract a mixed crowd.

El Varón Rampante, C Arias Montano 3, **T** 656 906 663. *1900-0200. Map 4, G3, p255* Just off the Alameda de Hércules, this bar (appropriately named 'the rampant male') and the adjacent one, El Bosque Animado, attract plenty of people who mingle outside on weekend evenings. The crowd is mixed at peak times, but is usually fairly solidly gay male.

Hércules Mítico, Alameda de Hércules 93. *1600-0400. Map 4, G3, p255* A popular bar on this long square with a tall and elegant trannie as host. Modern interior and largely gay male crowd; music is mostly recent Spanish pop hits, but there are some DJ nights with varying types of dance music.

Itaca, C Amor de Dios 31. *2300-0500. Map 4, I3, p255* Seville's best gay *discoteca*, always well-attended and with appropriately good dance music. There's a backroom and shows from Wed-Sat nights.

Men to Men, C Trajano 38. *2230-0500. Map 4, I2, p255* A gay club near the Alameda. Large, dark and popular with a dark room and decent dance music.

Monasterio, C Amor de Dios 18. *Thu-Sat 2300-0600. Map 4, I3, p255* Another decent *discoteca* with a principally gay and lesbian crowd.

Noveccento, C Julio César 10. *Winter 1700-0200, summer 2000-0400. Map 3, C7, p252* A bar and café that attracts a mixed crowd with a significant lesbian element. Frequent shows that cater to both guys and gals.

Why Not, C Federico Sánchez s/n, **T** 954 222 636. *Thu-Sat 2300-0500.* *Map 2, E2, p250* Relaxed *discoteca* with a mixed, but mostly gay male, crowd. There are three rooms, the first quiet and decorated with Hollywood icons and a bonsai tree. The two dance floors are fairly crowded and have good sound systems walloping out unchallenging popular hits that are enthusiastically received. Entry is €10 including drink; there's another branch at Calle Bedoya 20 and an outdoor one in summer behind the Plaza de Armas bus station.

Bookshops

Librería Amaranta, C Pérez Galdós 24. *Map 2, A5, p250* A gay oriented bookshop near Plaza Alfalfa.

Magazines and newspapers

A useful magazine is *Shanguide*, with reviews, events, information, and city-by-city listings for the whole country.

Organizations

Colega Andaluza, Plaza Encarnación 23, **T** 954 501 377. *Map 4, L4, p255* Seville branch of a nationwide gay and lesbian association.

Girasol, **T** 958 200 602. An Andalucía-wide lesbian and gay association based in Granada.

SOMOS, Plaza Giraldillo 1, **T** 954 531 399. *Map 1, C3, p248* A gay and lesbian support organization.

Saunas

Nordik, C Resolana 38, **T** 954 371 321. *Map 4, C4, p254*
Comfortable and well-equipped gay sauna in La Macarena.

Termas Hispalis, C Céfiro 3, **T** 954 580 220. *Map 1, H8,
p249* Another popular Seville sauna with plenty of people and
action.

Shops

Asuntos Internos, C Bailén 24, **T** 954 212 380. *Map 3, B8,
p252* A gay-friendly shop selling underwear and swimsuits
from the executive to the provocative.

Guappos, C Trastamara 29, **T** 954 216 537. *Map 3, D6, p252*
A similar shop, but with a larger range of clothing and accessories.

Websites

www.gayinspain.com/andalucia/Sevilla.htm
Extensive listings of bars, clubs, zones, etc

www.solodecontactos.com
Gay contacts by Spanish province.

www.colegaweb.net
The website of a national gay and lesbian association.

www.es.gay.com
National portal of principal use for contacts and chat.

Kids are kings in Spain and it's one of the easiest places to take them along on holiday. Children socialize with their parents from an early age here and you'll see them eating in restaurants and out in bars well after midnight. Children are basically expected to eat the same sort of things as their parents, although you'll sometimes see a *menú infantil* at a restaurant, which typically has simpler dishes and smaller portions than the norm. Few places, however, are equipped with high chairs, unbreakable plates, or baby-changing facilities.

Despite the positives, Seville's high summer temperatures and architectural glories may not impress the average kid, so you'll have to plan things a little. In terms of the two major festivals, Feria, with its horses and pageantry is a much better bet for the young than Semana Santa.

Activities

Football, see p187. The atmosphere at Spanish games is very unintimidating; a lot of families and children are present and there's no alcohol consumed. This is true for any game except the Betis-Sevilla local derby.

Isla Mágica, Isla de la Cartuja, by Puente de la Barqueta, **T** 902 161 716, www.islamagica.es *Apr-Oct (Tue-Sun until mid-Jul, then daily until mid-Sep, thereafter weekends only), 1100-1900 (2200 at weekends and in summer, 2400 in high summer). Entry €19-21, €13-14.50 kids and seniors, about 30% reduced if you enter after 1600. Bus C1, C2. Map 1, C3, p248* This theme park, roughly themed on Seville and the discovery of the Americas, has plenty for all and is big enough to be worth the entry fee.

Markets

The flea market in the Alameda de Hércules on Sunday mornings is fun to explore for young and old as is the Thursday morning market along Calle Feria nearby. *Map 4, G3, p255*

Sights

Parque María Luisa. *Daily 0800-2400 summer, 2200 winter. Free. Bus C1, C2, 30, 31, 33, 34. Map 2, L6, p251* A big, beautiful park with plenty of room to burn off energy and bikes for hire. See also p200.

Pabellón de la Energía Viva, C Marie Curie s/n, **T** 954 467 146, www.pabellondelaenergiaviva.com *Mon-Sat 1000-1900, Sun 1100-1900. €5.60. Bus C1, C2. Map 1, C2, p248* This newly-opened environmental museum has plenty of hands-on stuff that will appeal to kids of 12 and over. See also p88.

Kids

Shopping

Catedral Pibe, Av Luís Montoto 110. *Map 1, H8, p249*
Stylish footwear for kids.

Entre Arte, Paseo de Colón 19. *Map 3, H8, p253*
A shop selling dolls and dolls houses in a beautiful building
on the riverfront.

Junio Decor, C Juan Sebastian Elcano 14. *Map 2, L1, p251*
Must Seville fashion for kids.

Tours

The river trips on the Guadalquivir and the open-top bus trips
around town are entertaining and won't outlast attention spans.
The Carmen tour is also upbeat, fun, and interesting. See also p29.

Zoos

Carmona Zoo, **T/F** 954 19 16 96, www.zoocarmona.com
*1000-dusk daily, except high summer 1500-1800. Phone to check
opening times as they change frequently. €2.40 kids, €3 adults.
Off main road between Seville and Carmona.* Focusing mostly on
Spanish animals, most of which have been rescued from accident
or misfortune, Carmona Zoo has a particularly educational slant.

Jerez Zoo, C Taxdirt, **T** 956 18 23 97, **F** 956 31 15 86,
www.zoobotanicojerez.com *Tue-Sun 1000-dusk. €2.61 (3-13
year olds), €3.98 adults.* Situated on the northwestern outskirts
of the city, this is one of the country's best zoos and features all
the favourite animals, including a rare white tiger.

Kids

Airline offices
Iberia, Av Buhaira 8, **T** 954 988 208 / 902 400 500. *Mon-Fri 0900-1330; 1600-1900.* **Air Europa**, Aeropuerto San Pablo, **T** 954 449 179. **Air France**, Aeropuerto San Pablo, **T** 954 449 252.

Banks and ATMS
There are banks all over the place, all with ATMs that accept Cirrus, Maestro, Visa, MasterCard and most other international credit and debit cards. If you need an exchange, banking hours are Mon-Fri 0900-1400 and Sat 0900-1300 (only in winter months). Outside these hours, you can change money at major hotels or El Corte Inglés department store at murderous rates. Better is the Amex office by the Hotel Inglaterra on Plaza Nueva.

Bicycle hire
Bicicletas Astolfi, Av Fedriani 35, **T** 954 389 272, www.bicicletas-astolfi.com Good quality bikes for rent at €12 per day. **Cyclotour**, Parque María Luisa. Pricey, but fun, shaded two and four seater rickshaws for hire at €10 per hr for a two seater or €12 for a four seater. **Quiquecycle**, Parque María Luisa. Simple but reasonable bikes for hire at €3 per hour.

Car hire
Major international firms at the airport: **Budget**, **T** 954 999 137 and **Hertz**, **T** 954 514 720. **Avis**, **T** 954 537 861, has an office at the train station. Better-value local firms can be found on and near Calle Almirante Lobo by the Torre del Oro. These include **Atlantic**, **T** 954 227 893, **ATA**, **T** 954 220 957 and **Sevilla Car**, **T** 954 222 587. Another reasonable agency is **Hispalis**, C García de Vinuesa 22, **T** 954 226 833, www.autoshispalis.com

Consulates
See the tourist office for a fuller list. **Australia**, C Federico Rubio 14, **T** 954 220 971. **Belgium**, C Bilbao 12, **T** 954 229 090. **Britain**,

Urbanización Aljamar, Tomares, **T** 954 155 018. **Denmark**, Av Palmera 19, **T** 954 296 819. **France**, Pl Santa Cruz 1, **T** 954 222 896. **Germany**, Av Palmera 19, **T** 954 230 204. **Morocco**, Con Descubrimientos s/n, **T** 954 081 044. **Netherlands**, C Placentines 1, **T** 954 228 750. **USA**, Paseo Delicias 7, **T** 954 231 885.

Credit Card lines

Amex: **T** 902375637; **MasterCard**: **T** 900971231; **Visa**: **T** 900951125.

Dentists

There are numerous dentists; the tourist office can help locate one. For emergencies there's a rotating roster of dentists, so call **T** 902 505 061, the general number for health emergencies in Andalucía.

Disabled

CEADIS, C Fray Isidoro de Seville 1, **T** 954 915 444, can put you in touch with a wider support network.

Doctors

For an emergency, see below. There are numerous Centros de Salud. Central ones: **El Cachorro**, C Castilla s/n, Triana, **T** 954 330 000 and **Nuestra Señora de los Reyes**, Av Marqués de Paradas 18, **T** 954 248 950. In all cases you'll need a copy of Form E111 (EU residents; available from post offices in Britain) or proof of coverage if you don't want to pay.

Electricity

Spain runs on 220V, as does most of Europe, with a two-pin plug.

Emergency numbers

General emergencies, call **T** 112. For police, **T** 091 (**T** 092 for local police, who deal in everyday matters), for an ambulance, **T** 061. For reporting crimes on **T** 902 102 112.

Hospitals

For minor medical emergencies, by far the best and handiest centre is: **Centro El Porvenir**, Av Menéndez Pelayo 33, **T** 954 421 861, opposite the Jardines de Murillo. Full scale hospitals include: **Hospital La Macarena**, Av Doctor Fedriani 3, **T** 955 008 000. **Hospital Virgen del Rocío**, Av Manuel Siurot s/n, **T** 955 012 000.

Internet/email

There are dozens of options in Seville, most around the €1.80-€2.50 mark. **Workcenter**, C San Fernando 1, **T** 954 212 074, also Av Reina Mercedes 15, **T** 954 238 292. Open daily 24 hrs ; access is reasonable and costs €2 per hr. **Seville Internet Center**, Av Constitución 24, 2º, digital photo services too, expensive at €3 per hour, flat screens, Mon-Fri 0900-2200, Sat-Sun 1000-2200.

Language schools

There are many options. Some with good reputations include: **Instituto de Estudias de la Lengua Española (IELE)**, C García de Vinuesa 29, **T** 954 560 788, www.iele.com Current prices are €360 for 4 weeks at 15 hrs a day, €480 at 20 a day. **Lenguaviva**, C Viriato 24, **T** 954 905 131, www.lenguaviva.es Offers crash courses as well as more leisurely options. **CLIC**, C Albareda 19, **T** 954 502 121, www.clic.es. Lively teaching, accommodation and excursions. Youngish set. **Linc**, General Polavieja 13, **T** 954 500 459, www.linc.tv Centrally located school with a variety of courses.

Laundrettes

Lavandería Aguilas, C Aguilas 21, Mon-Fri 1000-2030, Sat 1000-1400. Self service and bag wash, between Plaza Alfalfa and the Casa de Pilatos. €7.20 service wash, €6.20 self service. **Lavandería Robledo**, C Federico Sánchez Bedoya 18ª, **T** 954 218 132. Mon-Fri 1000-1400, 1700-2000, Sat 1000-1400. €5.90 wash and dry. **Vera**, C Arjona 2. **Lavasolo**, Pasaje los Azahares off Plaza de San Andrés, **T** 954 216 356.

► Queipo de Llano

One of the Spanish Civil War's more interesting characters, Gonzalo Queipo de Llano was a former Republican sympathizer who had been a daring cavalry officer in Cuba and Morocco. Joining the conspiracy against the government, he went to Seville to oversee the military rising there. Finding the local garrison with loyalist tendencies, he astonishingly managed to bluff his way into taking the city with only 150 men, although fighting continued in Triana, which was later brutally taken with the help of troops flown over from Morocco.

Despite these events, and his successful capture of Málaga, he was most famous for his nightly radio broadcasts in which he harangued the Republican "rabble". The Marxists," he said "are ravening beasts, but we are gentlemen". Hardly, as the number of executions of civilians in the city was frightening; probably 10,000 or more, although Queipo himself was a much kinder-hearted man than his co-conspirators Franco and Mola.

His humorous radio rants both galvanized and cheered the Nationalists and reduced the Republicans to laughter. Accused of being drunk on air, he retorted "And why not? Why shouldn't a real man enjoy the superb quality of the wine and women of Sevilla?"

Perhaps not surprisingly, he wasn't taken seriously by Franco, and was deeply hurt when left out of the command council, whereupon he ceased his broadcasts, and closed a curious chapter of war history.

Left luggage

There are *consignas* at both bus stations and the train station, which has both automatic lockers and left luggage.

Lost property

There's a lost property office at C Manuel Vásquez Sagastizábal 3, **T** 954 420403. Mon-Fri 0700-1400.

Motorcycle hire

Alkimoto, C Fernando Tirado 5, corner of Luís Montoto, **T** 954 584 927, rents bikes €6 a day, scooters €21 or €70 for a week, or more serious bikes at decent rates. €6 delivery and take-away service to hotel. Also workshop. **Rentamoto**, C Padre Méndez Casariego 19, **T** 954 417 500, www.rentamoto.net €21 per day for a 49cc machine, €30 for a 125cc. Discounts for hire of 3 days or more. Near the Santa Justa train station.

Media

The press is generally of a high journalistic standard. The national dailies *El País*, *El Mundo* and the rightist *ABC* are accompanied by the local *Diario de Seville*. The sports dailies *Marca* and *As*, dedicated mostly to football, have an extremely large readership. The main television channels are the state-run TVE1, with standard programming, and TVE2, with a more cultural/sporting bent alongside the private *Antena 3*, *Tele 5* and *Canal Plus*. There's also a local Andalucían station. The kiosk on Calle Velázquez in the main shopping zone has a particularly wide selection of foreign papers.

Pharmacies (late night)

Pharmacies are everywhere and the staff highly qualified. They take it in turns to open at weekends and at night. Every pharmacy has the current roster posted in the window (*farmacías de guardia*), as do the local newspapers.

Police

Dial **T** 091 for a police emergency, **T** 092 to speak to the local police. The handiest police station is on Calle Betis s/n, on the Triana riverfront side, halfway along.

Post offices

The main post office is on Av de la Constitución 32, **T** 902 197 197. There's also one in Triana on the corner of Calles San Jacinto and Pagés del Corro. They're open Mon-Fri 0830-2030, and Sat 0930-1400. Stamps (*sellos*) can be bought only at post offices or tobacconists (*estancos*). A letter to the EU costs €0.51.

Public holidays

Año Nuevo, New Year's Day (1 Jan), **Reyes Magos/Epifania**, Epiphany, when Christmas presents are given (6 Jan). Easter **(Semana Santa):Jueves Santo, Viernes Santo, Día de Pascua** (Maundy Thursday, Good Friday, Easter Sunday). **Día de Andalucía**, Andalucía Day (28 Feb). **Fiesta de Trabajo**, Labour Day (1 May). **Asunción**, Feast of the Assumption (15 Aug). **Día de la Hispanidad**, Spanish National Day, Columbus Day, Feast of the Virgin of the Pillar (12 Oct). **Todos los Santos**, All Saints Day (1 Nov). **El Día de la Constitución Española**, Constitution Day (6 Dec). **Inmaculada Concepción**, Feast of the Immaculate Conception (8 Dec). **Navidad**, Christmas Day (25 Dec).

Religious services

Roman Catholic mass times are posted on the doors of churches. There's a Presbyterian church at C Huesca 13, **T** 954 640 577. The IERE is a Spanish Episcopalian group with a church at Calle Relator 45, **T** 954 388 725 and mass at 1100 on Sun.

Taxi firms

Tele Taxi, **T** 954 622 222. **Radio Taxi**, **T** 954 583 605.

Telephone

International dialling code is +34. To make an international call from Spain, dial 00 followed by the country code. Calls within Spain begin with a three digit area code (eg Seville is 954); this must be dialled in all cases. Mobile numbers begin with 6. Public phones accept coins and cards and all have international direct dialling, although you'll save money by buying a prepaid card (*tarjeta telefónica prepagada*) from a kiosk. Cheap phone calls can also be made from *locutorios* (call centres): C Pastor y Landero 15, opposite the Arenal market, the corner of Calle Apante and Calle Trajano just off Plaza del Duque.

Time

Spain is one hour ahead of GMT and puts its clocks forward and back at the same time as Britain and the rest of Europe.

Toilets

Public toilets are few, but most bars won't have a problem with you using theirs, as long as you ask. Few have locks or paper. *Caballeros* (occasionally *Señores*) is men and *Señoras* is girls. Toilets are indicated by any of the following: *Aseos*, *Baños*, *Servicios* or *HHSS*.

Transport enquiries

Trains: RENFE, **T** 902 240 202. **Airport**: **T** 954 449 000. **Plaza de Armas bus station**: **T** 954 908 040. **Prado de San Sebastián bus station**: **T** 954 417 111. There's a handy central RENFE office to book train tickets at C Zaragoza 29.

Travel agents

Asatej, C O'Donnell 3, 3rd floor, **T** 902 444 488, www.asatej.es A competent agency specializing in youth/student travel. **Viajes Halcón**, Av Constitución 5, **T** 902 433 000. **Viajes Ecuador**, Av Constitución 4, **T** 902 207 070. **Viajes El Monte**, C Martín Vila 4, **T** 954 211 111. **Távora Viajes**, C Zaragoza 1, **T** 954 226 160.

A sprint through history

6000-3000 BC	Neolithic period. The first settlements in the area appear. Associated evidence of agriculture, domestication and ceramic production is found.
3000-1100	Chalcolithic period and Bronze Age with working of copper followed by alloys. The Guadalquivir river valley itself is probably still only used seasonally due to flooding.
1100-700	The Tartessian civilization develops with ironworking and the expansion of cities. While Seville legend attributes the founding of the city to Hercules, it is very possible that the Tartessians built the first permanent settlements on this site, although there is little concrete evidence.
700-500	The establishment of Phoenician, and later, Greek trading colonies on the Andalucían coast enables a rich cultural interchange with the Tartessians, who became skilled goldsmiths and developed writing and extensive trading. The Phoenicians establish a settlement in Seville and extend and fortify the city.
500-206	The Turditanians inherit Tartessian culture. Strife with the Phoenicians leads to a Carthaginian takeover of the city, which, however, continues to be an important trading centre for the western Mediterranean.

206 BC	The Romans arrive, defeat the Carthaginians at the battle of Ilipa and establish Itálica on high ground near Seville, which they named Hispalis. The river was known as the Betis.
69-45 BC	Julius Caesar arrives, first as an administrator, then becoming governor of the province. He liked Hispalis, particularly after its citizens sided with him against Pompey, and he conferred full Roman citizenship on the inhabitants.
27 BC	Hispalis is made capital of the large southern province of Baetica.
AD 1st-4th centuries	A period of prosperity and relative peace as Itálica and Hispalis are both important Roman cities. Little remains in Seville of the Roman period, but Itálica preserves the hallmarks of a major centre. Trajan was born there and Hadrian grew up there, as did several notable writers and orators. Christianity took early root in Hispalis and, after early persecutions, soon flourished.
AD 426-711	Vandals and Swabians sack the city as the Roman Empire collapses. The Visigoths are more cultured visitors and respect local traditions. The city flourishes under their rule and the wise archbishops Leandro and Isidoro, a scholar-saint who was one of the most important intellectual figures of the Middle Ages. His prolific writings covered all subjects and were still popular at the time of the Renaissance.

711	The Islamic invasion puts an end to the Visigothic kingdom. Hispalis is renamed Isbiliyya, from which Seville is derived. The river is renamed *al wadi al kibir* (big river), or Guadalquivir as it is now written.
756	The Córdoba caliphate is declared and Isbiliyya commences a long period under its neighbour's shadow.
844	The Vikings, impressively, are surprise visitors up the river. They sack the city comprehensively as was their horned-helmeted wont.
1023	After the collapse of the Córdoba caliphate, Isbiliyya declares itself an independent *taifa* state, and rapidly becomes the most powerful in Al-Andalus, the Moorish dominions.
1068-1091	Under the poet-king Al-Mutamid, the city and its Muslim, Jewish and Christian population, experiences an exceptional flourishing of wealth and the arts.
1091	The hardline Almoravids take the city but soon assimilate.
1147	The Almohads take Isbiliyya and start making important improvements. The city walls and the Torre del Oro all date from this period, as does the Great Mosque, now Seville's cathedral.
1248	Isbiliyya is conquered by the Castillian king Fernando III and nearly all its Muslim population is expelled. Their lands are divided among noble families.

1280	Alfonso X thanks the city for its support for him against his son Sancho, and adds "No me ha dejado (you didn't forsake me) to the city's arms. Transformed into a rebus, (NO DO with a skein of wool – *madeja* – in the middle), this is still the city's motto, and seen everywhere.
1350-69	Pedro I, an enlightened and curious character, somewhat unfairly nicknamed "the Cruel", loves the city and has the Alcázar rebuilt in sumptuous Mudéjar style.
1391	A massive anti-Jewish pogrom in the city. Synagogues are forcibly changed into churches and the Jewish quarter virtually ceases to exist.
1401	Work on the cathedral is started.
1492	Under the patronage of the Roman Catholic Monarchs, Fernando and Isabel, Christopher Columbus "discovers" America. This marks the beginning of Seville's golden age; in 1503 it is granted a monopoly on trade with the New World, and becomes one of the largest and most prosperous cities in Europe.
1519	Ferdinand Magellan sets sail from Triana attempting a circumnavigation of the world. He didn't make it, but one of his ships, skippered by Juan Sebastián Elkano, did, arriving three years later.
17th century	The first decades of the 17th century mark the zenith of the Seville school of painting, with artists such as Zurbarán, Murillo, and Velásquez all operating. However, the Spanish crown, over-

committed to wars on all fronts, sinks further into economic crisis. The expulsion of the *moriscos* (converted Moors) in 1610 hit the city hard and merchants pack up and move on, leaving Seville in an increasingly desperate state. A plague in 1649 kills an incredible half of the inhabitants and the decline is rapid.

1717 As the Guadalquivir becomes increasingly unnavigable, New World trade is officially transferred to Cádiz.

1810-1812 French occupation of Seville results in some much-needed modernization but also much pillaging of artworks from monasteries.

1836 Church property is appropriated by the state, creating more public space in Seville but also favouring rich landowners, who bought up estates at bargain prices.

1910 The CNT, an important anarchist confederation, is founded in the city which has very strong anarchist traditions.

1929 The Ibero-American exhibition is opened in Seville. The preparation for this lavish event effectively created the modern city we know today, and, despite bankrupting the city, set the framework for a 20th century urban centre.

1936-39 The Spanish Civil War. The oddball general Queipo de Llano bluffs his way into control of the city. Workers struggle against the rising and are brutally repressed with much of Triana destroyed.

1982	A *sevillano*, Felipe González, is elected as the first Socialist prime minister since before the Civil War. He governs until 1996. The city hosts a World Cup semi-final in a big year for Spain.
1992	Another big year for Spain. Olympics in Barcelona and Seville, now the capital of semi-autonomous Andalucía, hosts World Expo 1992. This event attracts some 15 mn visitors and leaves the city with enormous debts.
2003	Boosted by much post-Expo tourism, the city continues its urban improvements with a Metro under development and the new Olympic stadium hosting the UEFA Cup final. Unemployment, poverty and homelessness continue to be massive, if not particularly visible, problems.

Art and architecture

First millennium BC

The Tartessians, inspired by their contact with the Phoenicians and Greeks, produce some exquisite gold jewellery, a large hoard of which was found at El Carambolo near Seville. Various Phoenician pieces have also been found, notably a votive icon of the goddess Astarte now in Seville's Archaeological museum. Almost no architectural traces remain in the Seville area from this period, although Carmona's impressive bastion preserves its Phoenician foundations.

Roman Period 206 BC-AD 426

Although Seville was an important Roman city, subsequent construction has left little from the period. Excavations at nearby Itálica, however, have revealed an extensive Roman city, with numerous fine examples of sculpture and mosaics unearthed, mostly dating from the second and third centuries AD, as the older part of Itálica is still under the village of Santiponce. Carmona preserves an important Roman necropolis.

Visigothic Period 426-711

While Seville was for a time the Visigothic capital, almost nothing remains from this period.

First Taifa Period 1023-1091

After the fall of the Córdoba caliphate, Isbiliyya (Seville) emerged from the shadows to become the most important city in Muslim Spain. The Alcázar is constructed in Seville.

Almohad Period 1147-1248

Nearly all of Seville's Moorish architectural heritage dates from this period. The Almohads fortify the city, building simple, attractive, and effective walls and towers, including the Torre del Oro, a jewel of military architecture. The city's great mosque was built where the cathedral now stands. Little remains of this but the orange-tree courtyard, a gate, and the design of the Giralda, once the mosque's mighty minaret. *Azulejos*, the colourful painted tiles so typical of Seville, were first used during this period, as was the ornamental brickwork that also characterized later "Mudéjar" architecture. Fabulous inlaid wooden ceilings were another innovation that was continued and developed for many more centuries.

Gothic-Mudéjar Period 1248-early 16th century

With the Christian conquest, the pointed style beginning to make its mark in the north was brought to Seville. It was combined with styles learned under the Moors to form an Andalucían fusion known as Gothic-Mudéjar. Many of Seville's churches are constructed on these lines, typically featuring a rectangular floor plan with a triple nave surrounded by pillars, a polygonal chancel and square chapels. Gothic exterior buttresses were used, and many had a bell tower decorated with ornate brickwork reminiscent of the Giralda, which was also rebuilt during this period after earthquake damage. The Alcázar built by Pedro I is an imaginative fusion of Christian and Muslim traditions; Seville's cathedral is much purer Gothic in style, and started in the early 15th century.

**16th and
17th
centuries**

Seville was understandably one of the centres of the Spanish Renaissance, as the Americas were discovered, and wealth seemed limitless. The ornamental late-Gothic Isabelline style led to the Plateresque, a word that refers particularly to the façades of buildings, decorated with shields and other heraldic motifs, as well as geometric and naturalistic patterns. Seville's *Ayuntamiento* is a supreme example of this.

A classical revival put an end to much of the elaboration, as architects began to concentrate on purity and imported classical Greek features such as pediments and Italian cupolas and domes. Elegant interior patios, always a feature of Muslim architecture in Seville, became popular again. Seville has much fine Renaissance architecture – the Casa de Pilatos is an exceptional example, while the Archivo de las Indias is a demonstration of the more sober Renaissance style.

This was also the great period of Sevillian painting; artists such as Pedro de Campaña, Velásquez, Zurbarán, and Murillo and sculptors of the calibre of Juan Martínez Montañés lifted Spanish art to unprecedented heights. Seville's cathedral, art gallery, and various churches and hospitals around the town are replete with works by these and other masters.

**The
baroque**

As Seville declined, the artistic and architectural focus moved away from it, but there are numerous fine examples of baroque art and architecture in the city, particularly churches with their colourful ceramic belltowers (Ecija boasts some excellent examples) and ornate *retablos*. Churrigueresque refers to the intricate extreme of this style, typically featuring *solomónica* (Solomonic or corkscrew) columns and pilasters decorated with tendrils and cherubs. Many of Seville's Semana Santa sculptures are from this period, a medium in which the style is seen as its best, as it is capable of expressing intense emotion.

Neo-classical 18th and 19th centuries The neoclassical period was a severe reaction to the ornamentality of the baroque and sought a return to purity of form. Plazas were opened up and façades became simpler interplays of angles. A perfect example is the front of the *Ayuntamiento* and the Plaza Nueva.

Early 20th century The 1929 exhibition saw an architectural revival as sumptuous neo-Moorish pavilions were erected alongside the grandiose, but harmonious Plaza de España. Seville's new town was opened up along wide avenues and the city took its modern shape.

Post-Franco After the architectural stagnation of the Franco years, Seville was given the opportunity to showcase modern ideas with the 1992 Expo. As well as the many fine pavilions, the most endearing legacy is the fluid, river bridges by Calatrava. The impressive Teatro de la Maestranza, public library, and renovation of the Casa de las Monedas also date from around this time. The monastery of La Cartuja is now a gallery for modern Andalucían art, which as yet is not given as high a profile as in other parts of the country.

Books

Fiction

Cohen, J (ed), *The Penguin Book of Spanish Verse.* (1988), Penguin. Excellent collection of Spanish poetry through the ages with original versions and transcriptions.

Pérez-Reverte, A, *The Seville Communion.* (1995), Harvill. Entertaining novel of renegade priests and shifty Seville characters who spend their time in various well-known cafés and tapas bars.

Non-fiction

Ball, P, *Morbo.* (2001), WSC Books. Entertaining review of rivalry in Spanish football with plenty to say on Sevilla-Betis.

Ford, R, *A Hand-Book for Travellers in Spain.* (1845), John Murray Press. Difficult to get hold of (there have been several editions) but worth it; amazingly comprehensive and entertaining guide written by a 19th century British gentleman who spent five years in Spain. There is much information on Seville.

Ford, R, *Gatherings from Spain.* (1846), John Murray Press. Sweeping overview of Spanish culture and customs; Richard Ford was something of a genius and has been surpassed by few, if any, travel writers since. Recently reprinted by Pallas Athene.

Hemingway, E, *Death in the Afternoon.* (1939), Jonathan Cape. Excellent book on bullfighting by a man who fell heavily for it. Lengthy descriptions of the great Seville fighters.

Jacobs, M, *Andalucía*. (1998), Pallas Athene. An excellent series of essays and information by a British writer who knows the region deeply.

Ros, C, *Desde El Balcón de la Giralda*. (1991), Rodríguez Castillejo. Charming anecdotes in Spanish about various incidents involving kings, archbishops and locals of Seville over the centuries.

Sánchez Montero, R, *A Short History of Seville*. (1992), Sílex Signos. Exactly what it says on the cover: succinct, readable and intelligent.

Thomas, H, *The Spanish Civil War*. (1961/77), Penguin. The first unbiased account of the war read by many Spaniards in the censored Franco years. Large but always readable. Plenty of material on wartime Seville. A well-researched work.

Woodall, J, *In Search of the Firedance*. (1992), Sinclair Stevenson. An excellent and impassioned history and travelogue of *flamenco*, if inclined to over-romanticize.

Language

Pronunciation

The stress in a Spanish word conforms to one of three rules: 1) if the word ends in a vowel, or in n or s, the accent falls on the penultimate syllable (*ventana, ventanas*); 2) if the word ends in a consonant other than n or s, the accent falls on the last syllable (*hablar*); 3) if the word is to be stressed on a syllable contrary to either of the above rules, the acute accent on the relevant vowel indicates where the stress is to be placed (*pantalón*). Unless listed below consonants can be pronounced in Spanish as they are in English.

b, v Their sound is interchangeable and is a cross between the English 'b' and 'v'; **c** Like English 'k', except before 'e' or 'i' when it is as the 'th' in English 'thimble'; **g** Hard like English 'game' or 'got' before 'a' or 'o', soft before 'e' and 'i' like the 'ch' in 'loch'; **h** Never pronounced except in combination 'ch' when it sounds like English chimney; **j** As the 'ch' in the Scottish 'loch'; **ll** As the 'y' in 'Yolanda' or the 'lli' in 'million'; **ñ** as the 'ni' in English 'onion'; **rr** Trilled much more strongly than in English; **z** As the 'th' in English 'thistle/thimble'

Greetings, courtesies

Hello/goodbye *hola/adios*
please/thank you (very much) *por favor/(muchas) gracias*
How are you? *¿Cómo está?/¿Cómo estás?*
Pleased to meet you *Encantado/encantada/mucho gusto*
What is your name? *¿Cómo se llama?*
Do you speak English? *¿Habla inglés?*
I don't speak Spanish *No hablo español*
I don't understand *No entiendo*
Please speak slowly *Hable despacio por favor*

Getting around

airport *el aeropuerto*
arrivals/departures *las llegadas/salidas*
Bus/train station *la estación de autobuses/de trenes*
corner *la esquina*
How do I get to_? *¿Cómo llego a_?*
near/far *cerca/lejos*
on the left/right *a la izquierda/derecha*
straight on *todo recto/derecho*
one-way/return *de ida/de vuelta*
When does the next plane/train leave/arrive? *¿Cuándo sale/llega el próximo avión/el tren?*
I want a ticket to_ *Quiero un billete a_*
Where is_? *¿Dónde está_?*

Accommodation

Do you have a room for two people? *¿Tiene una habitación para dos personas?*
Can I see the room? *¿Podría ver la habitación?*
with shower/bath *con ducha/baño*
with two beds/a double bed *con dos camas/una cama matrimonial*
air conditioning/heating *aire acondicionado/calefacción*
toilet paper *el papel higiénico*

Shopping

open/closed *abierto/cerrado*
How much does it cost? *¿Cuánto cuesta?*
change *cambio*
cheap/expensive *barato/caro*
credit card *la tarjeta de crédito*
travellers' cheques *los cheques de viajero*
post office *correos*
postcards/stamps *postales/sellos*

Eating out

breakfast *desayuno*
lunch *almuerzo/comida*
dinner *cena*
a table for two *una mesa para dos personas*
Can I see the menu? *¿Podría ver la carta por favor?*
fixed price menu *menú del día*
dish of the day *plato del día*
combined dishes *platos combinados*
refreshment stall *chiringuito*
bill/check *la cuenta*
Is service included? *¿Está incluido el servicio?*
bread/butter/sandwich *pan/mantequilla/bocadillo*
fork *tenedor*
spoon *cuchara*
knife *cuchillo*
toilet/toilets *servicios/aseos*
men *señores/hombres/caballeros*
women *señoras/damas*

Food glossary

Food and tapas

aceite oil; aceite de oliva is olive oil
aceitunas olives, also sometimes called olivas. The best kind are *manzanilla*, particularly when stuffed with anchovy (rellenas con anchoas)
acelga beet/chard
adobo marinated fried nuggets usually of shark; delicious
aguacate avocado

ahumado smoked; tabla de ahumados is a mixed plate
  of smoked fish

ajo garlic; *ajetes* are young garlic shoots

ajo arriero a simple sauce of garlic, paprika and parsley

albóndigas meatballs

alcachofa artichoke

alcaparras capers

aliño a salad, often of egg or potato, with chopped onion,
  peppers, and tomato with salt, vinagar, and olive oil.

alioli a tasty sauce made from raw garlic blended with oil and egg
  yolk. Also called *ajoaceite*

almejas name applied to various species of small clams

alubias broad beans

anchoa preserved anchovy

añejo aged (of cheeses, rums, etc)

angulas baby eels, a delicacy that has become scarce and
  expensive. Far more common are gulas, false angulas made
  from putting processed fish through a spaghetti machine.
  Squid ink is used to apply authentic colouring

anís aniseed, commonly used to flavour biscuits and liqueurs

arroz rice; *arroz con leche* is a sweet rice pudding

asado roast; an *asador* is a restaurant specializing in
  charcoal-roasted meat and fish

atún blue-fin tuna

azúcar sugar

bacalao salted cod, either delicious or leathery

berberechos cockles

berenjena aubergine/eggplant

besugo red bream

bistek steak: *poco hecho* is rare, *al punto* is medium rare,
  regular is medium, *muy hecho* is well-done

bizcocho sponge cake or biscuit

bocadillo/bocata a crusty filled roll

bogavante lobster

223

bonito atlantic bonito, a small, tasty tuna fish

boquerones fresh anchovies, often served filleted in garlic and oil

botella bottle

brasa (a la) cooked on a griddle over coals, sometimes you do it
  yourself at the table

brochetas de pescado fish kebab

buey ox

cabrales A pungent cheese from Asturias, similar in style to
  Roquefort

cabrito kid

cacahuetes peanuts

calamares squid

caldereta a stew of meat or fish usually made with sherry.
  Venao (venison) is commonly used, and delicious

caldo a thickish soup

callos tripe

cangrejo crab; occasionally river crayfish

caracol snail; very popular in Seville: *cabrillas*, *burgaos*,
  and *blanquillos* are popular varieties

caramelos sweets, popular with young and old

carne meat; *carne de vaca* beef

carillada the cheek and jowls of the pig or cow

castañas chestnuts

cazuela a stew, often of fish or seafood

cebolla onion

centollo spider crab

cerdo pork

ceviche shellfish salad marinated in lime juice

champiñon mushroom

chipirones small squid, often served in its own ink
  (*en su tinta*) deliciously mixed with butter and garlic

choco cuttlefish

chorizo a red sausage, versatile and of varying spiciness

chuleta/chuletilla chop

chuletón a massive T-bone steak, often sold by weight

churrasco barbecued meat, often ribs with a spicy sauce

churro a fried dough-stick usually eaten with hot chocolate,

chocolate con churros sually eaten as a late afternoon snack,
  merienda, but sometimes for breakfast.

cigala the four-wheel drive of the prawn world, with pincers

cochinillo roast suckling pig

cocido a heavy stew, usually of meat and chickpeas/beans
  Sopa de cocido is the broth, served first

codorniz quail

cogollo lettuce heart

cogollos con anchoa crisp lettuce hearts perked up with an anchovy

conejo rabbit

congrio conger-eel

cordero lamb

corvina meagre fish

costillas ribs

crema catalana a lemony crème brûlée

croquetas deep-fried crumbed balls of meat, béchamel,
  seafood or vegetables

dátiles dates

dorada a species of bream (gilthead)

dulce sweet

embutido any salami-type sausage

empanada a savoury pie, either pasty-like or in large, flat tins
  and sold by the slice. *Bonito* is a common filling, as is ham,
  mince or seafood

ensalada salad; *mixta* is usually a large portion of a bit of
  everything, an excellent option

ensaladilla rusa russian salad, potato, peas, and carrots in
  mayonnaise

escabeche pickled in wine and vinegar

espárragos asparagus, white and usually canned

espinacas spinach

estofado braised, often in stew form

fabada the most famous of Asturian dishes, a hearty stew of beans, *chorizo*, and *morcilla*

fideuá a bit like a paella but with noodles

flambeado flambéed

flamenquín a fried and crumbed finger of meat stuffed with ham

flan the ubiquitous crème caramel, great when home made (*casero*), awful out of a plastic cup.

foie fattened gooseliver, often made into a thick gravy-like sauce

frambuesas raspberries

fresas strawberries

frito/a fried

fruta fruit

galletas biscuits

gambas prawns

garbanzos chickpeas, often served in *espinacas con garbanzos*, a spicy spinach dish which is a signature of Seville

gazpacho a cold, garlicky tomato soup, very refreshing

granizado popular summer drink, like a frappé fruit milkshake

guisado/guiso stewed/a stew

guisantes peas

habas broad beans, often deliciously stewed *con jamón* (with ham)

harina flour

helado icecream

hígado liver

hojaldre puff pastry

horno (al) oven (baked)

hueva fish roe

huevo egg

huevos à la flamenca eggs fried in a terracotta dish with a spicy mixture of tomato and ham

huevos de codorniz quails' eggs

ibérico see *jamón*; the term can also refer to other pork products *jamón* ham: *jamón de York* is cooked British-style ham, but much better is the cured *serrano*. *Ibérico* refers to ham from a breed of pigs that graze wild in western Spain and are fed partly on acorns, *bellotas*. Particular regions and villages are known for their hams, which can get mighty expensive

judías verdes green beans

langosta crayfish

langostinos king prawns

lechazo milk-fed lamb

lechuga lettuce

lengua de almendra a small tongue-shaped almond cake

lenguado sole

lentejas lentils

limón lemon

lomo loin, usually sliced pork

longaniza a long sausage, speciality of Aragón

lubina sea bass

macedonia de frutas fruit salad, usually tinned

macerado marinated

manchego Spain's national cheese; hard, whiteish and made from ewe's milk

mantequilla butter

manzana apple

mariscos shellfish

mechada (minced) meat

mejillones mussels

melocotón peach, usually canned and served in *almibar* (syrup)

melva mackerel, often served semi-dried

menestra a vegetable stew, usually served like a minestrone without the liquid. Vegetarians will be annoyed to find that it's often seeded with ham and bits of pork

menú a set meal, usually consisting of three or more courses, bread and wine or water

menudo tripe stew, usually with chickpeas and mint

merluza hake is to Spain as rice is to southeast Asia
miel honey
migas breadcrumbs, fried and often mixed with lard and
  meat to form a delicious peasant dish of the same name
mojama cured tuna meat
mollejas sweetbreads; ie the pancreas of a calf or lamb
montadito a small, toasted filled roll
morcilla blood sausage, either solid or semi-liquid
morro cheek: pork or lamb
mostaza mustard
naranja orange
nata sweet, whipped cream
natillas rich custard dessert
navajas razor-shells
nécora small sea crab, sometimes called a velvet crab
nueces walnuts
orejas ears, usually of a pig
ostra oyster
pan bread
panes tasty open sandwiches
parrilla grill; a *parrillada* is a mixed grill
pastel cake/pastry
patatas potatoes; often chips, *patatas fritas*.
  Bravas are with spicy sauce
pato duck
pavía a crumbed and fried nugget of fish
  usually *bacalao* or *merluza*
pavo turkey
pechuga breast (usually chicken)
perdiz partridge
pescado fish
pestiños an Arabic-style confection of pastry
  and honey, traditionally eaten during *Semana Santa*

pez espada swordfish

picadillo a dish of spicy mincemeat

picante hot, i.e. spicy

pichón squab

picos breadsticks

pimienta pepper

pimientos peppers, of which there are many kinds: *piquillos* are the trademark thin Basque red pepper, *padron* produces sweet green mini ones and Bierzo loves theirs stuffed *rellenos*.

pinchito de lomo a small pork kebab

piña pineapple

pipas sunflower seeds, a common snack

plancha (a la) grilled on a hot iron or fried in a pan without oil

plátano banana

pollo chicken

postre dessert

pringá a tasty paste of stewed meats usually eaten in a *montadito* and a traditional final tapa of the evening

puerros leeks

pulpo octopus, particularly delicious *a la gallega*, boiled *Galician* style and garnished with olive oil, salt, and paprika

puntillitas small fine prawns, often served crumbed

queso cheese

rabo de buey/toro oxtail

ración a portion of food served in cafés and bars. Check the size and order a half (*media*) if you want less

rana frog; *ancas de rana* is frogs' legs

rape monkfish/anglerfish

relleno/a stuffed

revuelto scrambled eggs, usually with mushrooms or seafood, often a speciality

riñones kidneys

Riñones al Jerez kidneys stewed in sherry

rodaballo turbot, pricey and toothsome

romana (à la) fried in batter

sal salt

salchichón salami

salmón salmon

salmorejo a delicious thicker version of *gazpacho*, often garnished with egg and ham

salpicón a seafood salad with plenty of onion and vinegar

San Jacobo a steak cooked with ham and cheese

sardiñas sardines, delicious grilled

seco dry

secreto a grilled or fried piece of pork loin

sepia cuttlefish

serrano see jamón

setas wild mushrooms

solomillo beef fillet steak cut from the sirloin bone, deliciously fried in whisky and garlic in Seville, *solomillo al whisky*

sopa soup

surtido de queso/jamón platter of cheeses or ham

tajines a Moroccan stew typically of lamb with a fruit such as plums or apples. Also the name of the conical dish used to make it

tarta tart or cake

ternera veal or young beef

tocino pork lard; *tocinillo de cielo* is an excellent caramelized egg dessert

tomate tomato

torrijas a *Semana Santa* dessert, bread fried in milk and covered in honey and cinnamon

tortilla a Spanish omelette, with potato, egg, olive oil and optional onion

tostada toast

trucha trout

urta the red-banded sea bream, common off the Cádiz coast

uva grape

venao/venado venison

verduras vegetables

vieiras scallops, also called *veneras*
yema a rich egg-based pastry
zanahoria carrot

Drink

agua (mineral con gas/sin gas) water (mineral sparkling/still)
cachaça a white cane spirit, much like white rum
café coffee: *solo* is black, served espresso-style, *cortado* adds a
   dash of milk, *con leche* more and *americano* is a long black coffee.
caña a draught beer
caipirinhas the national drink of Brazil, a mixture of cachaça (a
   white cane spirit), lime juice, crushed ice, limes and sugar
cava sparkling wine
cerveza beer
chocolate a popular afternoon drink; also slang for hashish
chupitos shooters (cocktails or straight spirits)
fino the classic dry sherry
leche milk
manzanilla the dry, salty sherry from Sanlúcar de Barrameda.
   Also, confusingly, camomile tea and the tastiest type of olive
mosto grape juice, a common option in bars
orujo a fiery grape spirit, often brought to add to black coffee if
   the waiter likes you
rebujito a weak mix of *manzanilla* and lemonade, consumed by
   the bucket load during *Feria*
reserva, Gran Reserva Crianza terms relating to the age of wines.
Gran Reserva is the oldest and finest, then *Reserva* and *Crianza*
sidra cider
té tea
vaso glass
vino (tinto, blanco) wine (red, white); *rosado* or *clarete* is
   rosé; a *tinto de verano* is mixed with lemonade and ice, a
   refreshing option
zumo juice, usually bottled and pricey

Architecture glossary

alcázar a Moorish fort

ambulatory a gallery round the chancel and behind the altar

apse a vaulted square or rounded recess at the back end of a church or chapel

archivolt decorative carving around the outer surface of an arch

art deco a style that evolved between the world wars, based on geometric forms

art nouveau a reaction against architectural rigidity at the end of the 19th century that introduced whimsical naturalistic motifs to building design

artesonado ceiling ceiling of carved wooden panels with Islamic motifs popular throughout Spain in the 15th and 16th centuries.

azulejo an ornamental ceramic tile

baldacchino an ornate carved canopy above an altar or tomb; typical of Galicia

baroque ornate architectural style of the 17th and 18th centuries

bodega a cellar where wine is kept or made; the term also refers to modern wineries and wine shops

buttress a pillar built into a wall to reinforce areas of greatest stress. A flying buttress is set away from the wall; a feature of Gothic architecture

capilla a chapel within a church or cathedral

capital the top of a column, joining it to another section, often highly decorated

castillo a castle or fort

catedral a cathedral, ie the seat of a bishop

chancel the area of a church which contains the main altar, usually at the eastern end

chapterhouse area reserved for Bible study in monastery or church

Churrigueresque a particularly ornate form of Spanish baroque, named after the Churriguera brothers

colegiata a collegiate church, i.e. one ruled by a chapter of canons

conjunto histórico a tourist-board term referring to an area of historic buildings

convento a monastery or convent

coro the area enclosing the choirstalls, often central and completely closed off in Spanish churches

crossing the centre of a church, where the "arms" of the cross join

cuisson points where the beams intersect in a coffered ceiling: frequently decorated with shields

ermita a hermitage or rural chapel

Gothic 13th to 15th century style formerly known as pointed style. Distinguished externally by pinnacles and tracery around windows. Gothic architecture lays stress on the presence of light

hospital in pilgrimage terms, a place where pilgrims used to be able to rest, receive nourishment and receive medical attention

iglesia church

lobed arch a Moorish arch with depressions in the shape of simple arches

lonja a guildhall or fish market

mihrab a central niche in a mosque, always aligned towards Mecca and the focus for worshippers' prayers

mocárabes small concave spaces in Moorish ceilings

modernista a particularly imaginative variant of art nouveau that came out of Catalunya; exemplified by Gaudí

monasterio a large monastery usually located in a rural area

monstrance a ceremonial container for displaying the host

mozarabic the style of Christian artisans living under Moorish rule

mudéjar the work of Muslims living under Christian rule after the reconquest, characterized by ornate brickwork

multifoil a word describing a type of Muslim-influenced arch with consecutive circular depressions

muralla a city wall

Moorish mirrors
Seville's past is still reflected in the arts and crafts on sale today.

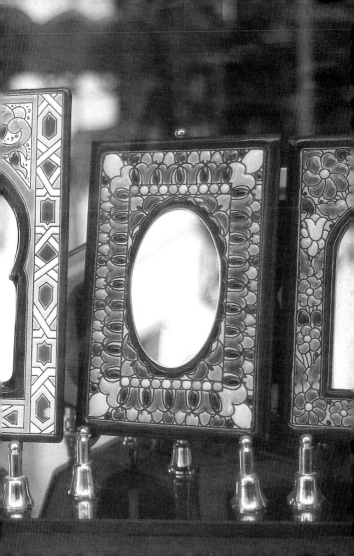

nave the main body of the church, a single or multiple
   passageway leading (usually) from the western end up
   to the crossing or high altar

neoclassical a reaction against the excesses of Spanish baroque,
   this 18th and 19th century style saw clean lines and symmetry
   valued above all things

palacio a palace or large urban or rural residence

patio an interior courtyard in a house, palace or mansion

pediment triangular section between top of columns and gables
   Curved section of cornice in baroque style

pilaster pillar attached to the wall

plateresque derived from *platero* (silversmith). Used to describe a
   uniquely Spanish Renaissance style characterised by finely carved
   decoration

reja ornate filigree screen, usually in churches

reliquary a container to hold bones or remains of saints
   and other holy things

Renaissance Spanish Renaissance architecture began when
   classical motifs were used in combination with Gothic
   elements in the 16th century

retablo altarpiece or retable formed by many panels often rising
   to roof level. Can be painted or sculptured

Romanesque (románico) style spread from France in the 11th and
   12th centuries, characterized by barrel vaulting, rounded apses
   and semicircular arches

romano roman; not to be confused with *románico*, which is
   Romanesque

sacristy (sacristía) part of Church reserved for priests to prepare
   for services

Solomónica a corkscrew column, a feature of late-Spanish
   baroque

soportales wooden or stone supports for the first floor of civic
   buildings, forming an arcade underneath

stucco (yesería) moulding mix consisting mainly of plaster
  Fundamental part of Muslim architecture
torre a tower
transept the short arms of a cross-shaped church
trascoro An ornate screen that closes off the back end of the *coro*
tympanum a space above a doorway but below its arch, often
  elaborately carved
vaulting support structure for roof. Romanesque buildings use
  barrel vaulting, a single curved constuction with no ribs. Gothic
  buidings use ribbed vaulting , four members meeting at a central
  point. Renaissance buildings use a more sophisticated forms of
  ribbed vaulting, such as aris, star or groin

General glossary

ayuntamiento a town hall
cante jondo the most serious and moving form of flamenco,
  a deep agonized lament about the cruelties of life
chicha a north-African hookah to smoke fruit tobacco
cofradía brotherhood
duende the dark, creative spirit of flamenco, also means
  goblin/imp
espartero coarse, hessian-like fabric woven from a tough grass
mantilla Lacy garment typical of Seville, worn by women either
  around the shoulders or, more formally, pinned to the back of
  the head with a *peineta* (large ornamental comb)
marcha good nightlife
movida a party or vibrant nightlife
Nazarenos hooded penitent
parador one of a chain of first-rate state-run hotels
pijo/a yuppie, used as a noun or adjective
rociera a form related to flamenco, songs whose subject
  is the annual pilgrimage to El Rocío over Whitsun.
taquilla ticket office

Index

Box index

Credits

Footprint credits
Editor: Claire Boobbyer
Map editor: Sarah Sorensen

Publisher: Patrick Dawson
Series created by Rachel Fielding
Cartography: Robert Lunn, Claire
Benison, Kevin Feeney, Shane Feeney
Design: Mytton Williams

Photography credits
Front cover: Charlie Newham, Alamy
(Alcázar)
Inside: Cathryn Kemp
(p1 Torre del Oro, p5 Jerez statue, p31
wrought-iron street lamp in Seville)
Generic images: John Matchett
Back cover: Cathryn Kemp

Print
Manufactured in Italy by LegoPrint.
Pulp from sustainable forests.

Footprint feedback
We try as hard as we can to make
each Footprint guide as up to date as
possible but, of course, things always
change. If you want to let us know
about your experiences – good, bad
or ugly – then don't delay, go to
www.footprintbooks.com and send
in your comments.

Publishing information
Footprint Seville
1st edition
Text and maps © Footprint
Handbooks Ltd November 2003

ISBN 1 903471 86 9
CIP DATA: a catalogue record for this
book is available from the British Library

Published by Footprint
6 Riverside Court
Lower Bristol Road
Bath, BA2 3DZ, UK
T +44 (0)1225 469141
F +44 (0)1225 469461
discover@footprintbooks.com
www.footprintbooks.com

Distributed in the USA by
Publishers Group West

Publishing stuff

Complete title list

Latin America & Caribbean

Argentina
Barbados (P)
Bolivia
Brazil
Caribbean Islands
Central America & Mexico
Chile
Colombia
Costa Rica
Cuba
Cusco & the Inca Trail
Dominican Republic
Ecuador & Galápagos
Guatemala
Havana (P)
Mexico
Nicaragua
Peru
Rio de Janeiro
South American Handbook
Venezuela

North America

Vancouver (P)
Western Canada

Middle East

Israel
Jordan
Syria & Lebanon

Africa

Cape Town (P)
East Africa
Egypt
Libya
Marrakech (P)
Marrakech &
 the High Atlas
Morocco
Namibia
South Africa
Tunisia
Uganda

Asia

Bali
Bangkok & the Beaches
Cambodia
Goa
Hong Kong (P)
India
Indian Himalaya
Indonesia
Laos
Malaysia
Myanmar (Burma)
Nepal
Pakistan
Rajasthan & Gujarat
Singapore
South India
Sri Lanka
Sumatra
Thailand
Tibet
Vietnam

Australasia

Australia
East Coast Australia
New Zealand
Sydney (P)
West Coast Australia

Europe

Andalucía
Barcelona
Berlin (P)
Bilbao (P)
Bologna (P)
Copenhagen (P)
Croatia
Dublin (P)
Edinburgh (P)
England
Glasgow
Ireland
Lisbon (P)
London
Madrid (P)
Naples (P)
Northern Spain
Paris (P)
Reykjavik (P)
Scotland
Scotland Highlands
 & Islands
Seville (P)
Spain
Turin (P)
Turkey
Verona (P)

(P) denotes pocket
Handbook

For a different view…
choose a Footprint

More than 100 Footprint travel guides
Covering more than 150 of the world's most exciting
countries and cities in Latin America, the Caribbean, Africa,
Indian sub-continent, Australasia, North America, Southeast Asia,
the Middle East and Europe.

Discover so much more…
The finest writers. In-depth knowledge. Entertaining and
accessible. Critical restaurant and hotels reviews. Lively
descriptions of all the attractions. Get away from the crowds.

What the papers say...

"I carried the South American Handbook from Cape Horn to Cartagena and consulted it every night for two and a half months. I wouldn't do that for anything else except my hip flask."
Michael Palin, BBC Full Circle

"My favourite series is the Handbook series published by Footprint and I especially recommend the Mexico, Central and South America Handbooks."
Boston Globe

"If 'the essence of real travel' is what you have been secretly yearning for all these years, then Footprint are the guides for you."
Under 26 magazine

"Who should pack Footprint–readers who want to escape the crowd."
The Observer

"Footprint can be depended on for accurate travel information and for imparting a deep sense of respect for the lands and people they cover."
World News

"The guides for intelligent, independently-minded souls of any age or budget."
Indie Traveller

Mail order
Available worldwide in bookshops and on-line. Footprint travel guides can also be ordered directly from us in Bath, via our website www.footprintbooks.com or from the address on the credits page of this book.

Check out...

100 travel guides, 100s of destinations, 5 continents
and 1 Footprint...

www.footprintbooks.com

Publishing stuff

Map 1 Seville

Map symbols

✈ Airport
🚌 Bus station
✚ Hospital
✉ Post office
†† Cathedral, church
✡ Synagogue
🏛 Museum
🎫 Tourist information
Ⓟ Police
P Parking
▸1 Detail map
◂1 Related map

0 metres 300
0 yards 300
N

Av Alcaide Manuel del Valle
C de San Juan de la C
C de San Juan de Aznalfarache Montero
Av de Llanes
C Samaniego
Estación de

Ronda Urbana N
Av de las Juventudes Musicales
Cementerio de San Fernando
C Doctor Fedriani
Parque del Alamillo
Av Concejal Alberto Jiménez Becerril
Puente del Alamillo
La Macarena
C Dr. Marañón
C José Díaz
C San Juan de Rivera
C Andueza
C Muñoz León
LA MACARENA
Plaza Ponce de León
Almirante C Escuelas
C María Auxiliadora
C Saturno

Puente de la Barqueta
C Resolana
C Calatrava
C Trajano
SAN VICENTE
Plaza Duque de la Victoria
C Baños
C Alfon

Isla Mágica
Pabellón de la Energía Viva
C Tomás Alva Edison
C Isaac Newton
C Marie Curie
Camino de los Descubrimientos
C Albert Einstein
C Charles Darwin
LA CARTUJA
Río Guadalquivir
C Torneo

Av de Carlos III
Monasterio de la Cartuja & Centro Andaluz de Arte Contemporáneo 🏛
Pasarela de la Cartuja

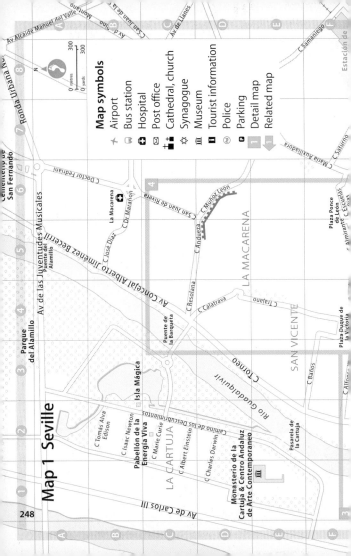

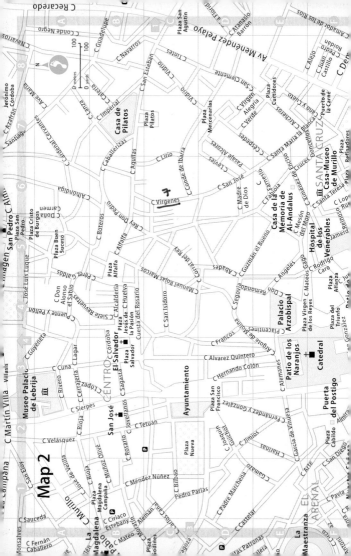

Map 3

252

Museo de Bellas Artes de Sevilla

La Magdalena

Plaza de Armas

Plaza del Museo

Río Guadalquivir

Av Cristo de la Expiación

Puente del Cachorro

Puente Isabel II (Puente de Triana)

Nuestra Señora de la O

Capilla de Patrocinio

Plaza Virgen de la Amargura

Paseo Cristób

Paseo Nuestra Señora de la O

Plaza Godines

Plaza Museo

Plaza Magdale Campana

C San Roque
C Monsalves
C Fernán Caballero
C Saucedo
C Vicente María
C Santa C
Concepc
Teñen
Buenos Libros
ler de
C Murillo
Pedro Parias,
C E Mar
C Carlos Canal
Plaza de la Legión
C Torremolinos
C Luis de Vargas
C Marqués de Paradas
C Trastámara
C Arjona
C Benidorm
C Sánchez
Barcaztegui
C Alhama
C Trastámara
C Reyes Católicos
C Gravina
C Julio César
C Canalejas
C Rafael Gonzáles Abreu
C Pedro Mártir
C Pedro del Toro
C Gravina
C Fray Diego de Deza
C Bailén
C Alfonso XII
Plaza
C Mendoza
C Red
C Marqué
C Abad Gordillo
C de la Ran
C San Pablo
C Ciriaco Estebany
C Mateo Alemán
C Zaragoza
C Santas Patronas
C Galera
C Pastor y Landero
C Almansa
C Genil
C Carenal
C Adriano
C Castelar
C Camino de
C Inca Garcilaso
C López Pintado
C Gonzalo Jiménez de Quesada
C Odiel
C Alfarería
C Gralla
C Chapina
C Alvarado
C Magallanes
C Pinzón
C Clara de Jesús Montero
C Procopedo
C Alfarería
C Castilla
C Tajares
C Termancia
C Numancia
C Uxama
C Virgen del Patrocinio
A B C D E F
1 2 3 4 5 6 7 8

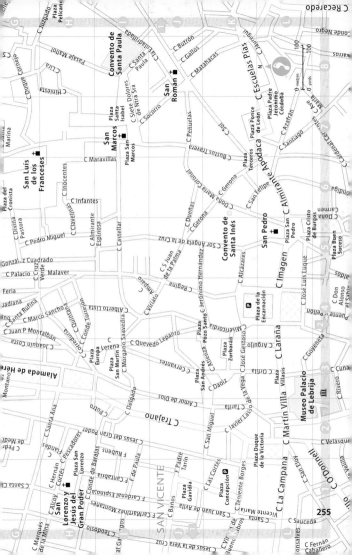

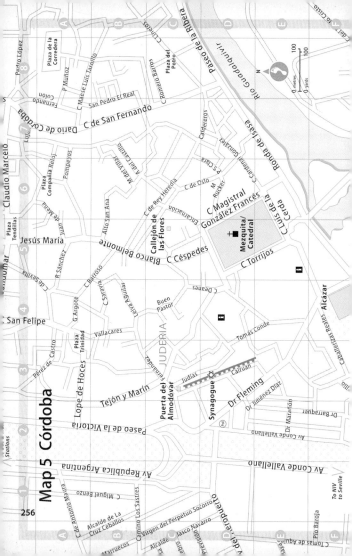

Map 5 Córdoba

256

Stations

A — Plaza de la Corredera

C Pedro López
C de Antonio Maura

C de Córdoba / Darío de Córdoba
Claudio Marcelo

Plaza de las Tendillas
Jesús María
Plaza Compañía Reloj
Plaza San Felipe

C de Sevilla

8 — P Muñoz
Matéo Luis Tavalillo
C Romero Barros
San Pedro El Real

C de San Fernando
Fernando Colón
Plaza del Potro

Pompeyos
M del Villar
A del Castillo
Alto San Ana
R Sánchez

Plaza Trinidad
C Saravia
Vallacares
C Barroso
G Argote

Pérez de Castro
Lope de Hoces
Tejón y Marín

Av República Argentina
C Miguel Benzo
Paseo de la Victoria

Alcalde de La
Cruz Ceballos
Camino Los Sastres
Alcalde
Virgen del Perpetuo Socorro

Paseo de la Ribera
C Linneros
Río Guadalquivir
Ronda de Isasa

Cardereros
P S Clara
Cardenal González

C de Oslo
M Rucker

C de Rey Heredia
Encarnación

Callejón de las Flores
Blanco Belmonte
C Céspedes
C Deanes
Buen Pastor

C Magistral
González Francés

Mezquita/Catedral

C Torrijos

Luis de la Cerda
Caballerizas Reales

Alcázar

JUDERIA

Puerta del Almodóvar

Judíos
Synagogue
Cairuan
Dr Fleming
Dr Jiménez Díaz

Tomás Conde

Av Conde Vallellano
Dr Marañón
Dr Conde Vallellano

Dr Barraquer

To NIV
to Seville

C Tomás de Aqui

Pío Baroja

N

0 metres   100
0 yards   100

Río Guadalquivir
C del Santo Cristo